Storytime

A 52-Week Bible Storybook for Families

Catherine DeVries

David C Cook
transforming lives together
www.davidccook.com

STORYTIME
Published by David C Cook
4050 Lee Vance View
Colorado Springs, CO 80918 U.S.A.

David C Cook Distribution Canada
55 Woodslee Avenue, Paris, Ontario, Canada N3L 3E5

David C Cook U.K., Kingsway Communications
Eastbourne, East Sussex BN23 6NT, England

LCCN 2013937393
ISBN 978-0-7814-0992-6

The Team: Catherine DeVries, Amy Konyndyk, Tonya Osterhouse
Cover Design: Amy Konyndyk

Manufactured in Kyonggi-do, Korea, in April 2013 by PACOM Korea Inc.
First Edition 2013

1 2 3 4 5 6 7 8 9 10

041713

Dear Parents,

In the busyness of each day, it can be difficult to set aside time with our families, let alone do devotions together. But you can accomplish both with *Storytime*.

I encourage you to find a regular time each week, maybe around the dinner table after a meal or before bed, to read this Bible storybook together. Make sure everyone is comfortable in a relaxed setting that will invite sharing.

This may feel awkward at first, but the structure of the book will soon help you establish a rhythm. Each of the 52 devotions begins with a Bible story, which is followed by a modern story, and then ends with family devotional time.

Family Talk Time is really the heart of this book. It's where you can remember and discuss the stories together, discover the Bible theme, and then share thoughts and experiences that relate to you personally as a family. Each Family Talk Time ends with a unique prayer and memory verse.

Invite your children to take turns reading the stories with you, if possible. They are written to be accessible to children as young as early readers. Try not to set a time limit for your family devotional time, but rather, let the Holy Spirit lead you to spend the time you need when you do this together.

As my husband and I have introduced this devotional structure in our own family, it has led to other "talk times" throughout the week. We have been blessed to see how God has been working in us. And I have also been touched by my youngest son's response to the experience. He just turned eight years old, and he loves reading the stories to us all by himself, fully participating. What a gift that is to our children—to invite them into the experience and even encourage them to take turns leading it.

One last thing! In order to help keep track of where you are from week to week, you may find it helpful to use a bookmark. You could even make one together as family!

May the Lord bless you and your family as you experience God and His Word through *Storytime*.

Sincerely,

Catherine DeVries

Storytime
Contents

We'd like to introduce you to the families in this book. They live in a nearby town and attend the same church. The children even all go to school together! Watch as their stories unfold, and see how these families and friends work together to live a Christian life as they face issues other families face today, including yours.

The Allen Family

Mr. Allen

Mrs. Allen

Michael

Munchkin

Mr. Allen, Mrs. Allen, Michael, and Munchkin are all part of this African-American family. Mr. Allen is a businessman, and Mrs. Allen is a librarian at the school that Michael, who is seven years old, and the other children attend. Munchkin, the bunny, is Michael's pet.

The Li Family

Dr. Li

Mrs. Li

Evan

Ava

Dr. Li and Mrs. Li moved to the United States from China. Dr. Li is a medical doctor. Mrs. Li is an artist. Their son, Evan, is five years old, and their daughter, Ava, is three years old.

The Lopez Family

Mrs. Lopez

Aunt Carla

Sophia

Alex

Slowpoke

Mrs. Lopez, Aunt Carla, Sophia, Alex, and Slowpoke are all members of the same Latino family. Sophia is six years old, and Alex, her five-year-old brother, has a pet turtle named Slowpoke.

The Mitchell Family

Mr. Mitchell

Caleb

Isaac

Nana Mitchell

The Mitchell family is made up of Mr. Mitchell, Caleb, Isaac, and Nana Mitchell. Mr. Mitchell is a single parent and a firefighter. Caleb is eleven years old, and Isaac is six years old. Nana lives in a different nearby town.

The Parker Family

Dr. Parker

Mrs. Parker

Brooke

Emma

Avery

Dr. Parker, Mrs. Parker, Brooke, Emma, and Avery are missionaries to India. Brooke is nine years old, Emma is six years old, and Avery is four years old.

The Scott Family

Mr. Scott

Mrs. Scott

Mia

Landon

Rascal

Peanut

The Scott family is made up of Mr. Scott, Mrs. Scott, Mia, her brother, Landon, and their pets, Rascal and Peanut. Mia is an Asian-Indian girl who was adopted by Mr. and Mrs. Scott. She is six years old. Landon is her two-year-old baby brother. Mr. Scott is a package delivery driver, and Mrs. Scott works as a day-care provider. Rascal is Mia's dog, and Peanut is her cat.

The Young Family

Mr. Young

Mrs. Young

Chloe

Madison

Kaden

Grandpa Young

Grandma Young

Pepper

Mr. Young, Mrs. Young, Chloe, Madison, Kaden, Grandpa Young, Grandma Young, and Pepper all make up this family. Mr. Young owns a sandwich shop. He and Mrs. Young teach Sunday school. Chloe is thirteen years old. She sometimes babysits. Madison and Kaden are twins who are six years old. Grandpa and Grandma Young live on a nearby farm and have a dog named Pepper.

God Made Day and Night

Bible story based on Genesis 1:1–5, 14–19

1. When God first made the world, it was dark everywhere. God said, "Let there be light." And there was light. He called the light "day." Later, God put the sun in the daytime sky. God said, "This is good."

2. God called the darkness "night." He put the moon and stars in the nighttime sky. God made the earth, sun, moon, and stars to mark off days, months, and years, and the four seasons. God looked at the light in the sky and said, "This is good."

At the Cabin

Aunt Carla and Sophia were spending the weekend at a cabin in the woods. All day long they walked through the trees and collected rocks. The sun shone brightly, and Sophia found many pretty rocks to show her family.

After dark it turned cool, so Aunt Carla made some hot cider. Sophia and Aunt Carla sat on the porch swing at the cabin. Before long, Sophia heard a funny noise: *Swish-swee, swosh-swee. Swish-swee, swosh-swee*.

"What's that?" Sophia asked.

Aunt Carla said, "It's the wind in the treetops. God made the trees and the wind."

Then Sophia heard *whip-poor-will, whip-poor-will*.

"What's that?" Sophia asked.

Aunt Carla said, "The birds are calling good night. God made the birds."

Next Sophia heard *crunch-chatter-chee, crunch-chatter-chee*.

"What's that?" Sophia asked.

Aunt Carla said, "It's a squirrel eating a nut. God made the squirrels and nuts."

Sophia liked all the new sounds she was hearing in the woods.

Aunt Carla said, "Look up, Sophia, and count the stars."

When Sophia thought she had counted all the stars, more seemed to appear.

Sophia asked, "Aunt Carla, did God make all the stars, too?"

"Yes," said Aunt Carla. "And He's watching over us right now."

As Sophia prayed before she got into bed, she thanked God for making the rocks, sunshine, trees, wind, birds, squirrels, nuts, and stars. And she said a special thanks that God was watching over her as she went to bed.

Family Talk Time

God Made Day and Night

Bible story based on Genesis 1:1–5, 14–19

As we begin to read this Bible storybook, let's go back to the very beginning when God created the world. He started by making day and night. He just told it to happen and it did!

Do you remember some of the things Sophia and Aunt Carla saw on their hike during the day? When it became dark outside and they were sitting on the porch at night, what did they hear? Isn't it amazing how there is always something we can discover, whether it is nighttime or daytime?

Get a flashlight and, as a family, sit together in one of your favorite rooms. If it's nighttime, have someone get up and turn off the lights. If it's daytime, make a "tent" out of a blanket and, with your entire family, climb inside. Click on the flashlight. Talk about your favorite things to do during the day. Now click off the flashlight (if this feels too scary, just keep it on). Talk about your favorite things to do during the night.

What We Learned about God: God made day and night.

Let's Pray: Dear God, thank You for making the day and the night. Each time of day is very different, and each time of day is very important. Thank You for all the fun things we can do during the day, and also for the things we can do at night, including getting our rest so we're ready for each new day. We can't wait to discover more about the world You made! Amen.

In the beginning God created the heavens and the earth.
Genesis 1:1

God Made Sky, Water, and Land

Bible story based on Genesis 1:1–10; Psalms 65:6–7; 135:7; Amos 4:13

God made the space above the earth and called it the "sky." God made the air, the clouds, and the wind in the sky.

God made water and land to be separate from each other. God said, "Let the water be gathered into one place. Let dry ground appear." And that's exactly what happened. God called the dry ground "land." He called the waters "sea."

The sea now covered only part of the earth instead of all the earth. God made the land have flat areas, gentle rolling hills, and mountains. God made the sand, soil, and rocks that cover the land.

God saw that the sky, water, and land that He had made were good.

Everything God Made

The Parkers were missionaries to India. They spent their time telling the people in India about God's love.

Mr. and Mrs. Parker, Brooke, Emma, and Avery had come home for a visit. Now they were flying back to India.

Avery fell asleep as soon as she got on the plane. But Brooke and Emma wanted to look out the window and see all the things God made.

Brooke said, "I can see twisty, turning rivers."

Emma said, "I can see big, rolling hills."

"Look," said Brooke. "There's the ocean. The water is so blue. And the ocean is so big that I can't see the end of it."

Then Emma said, "I can't see the rivers or the hills or the ocean anymore. All I can see is clouds. They look like giant cotton balls." The big silver airplane was up above the clouds.

Brooke read a book and Emma colored a picture. After eating supper on funny little trays, they both took a nap.

Much later Brooke looked out the window. "We're below the clouds now," she said.

Emma said, "I can see the edge of the big blue ocean. We're almost back in India."

Brooke said, "I can see twisty, turning rivers."

"And I can see big, rolling hills," said Emma.

Brooke asked, "Did God make the hills and rivers on this side of the ocean too?"

"Yes," said Dr. Parker. "God made them in India, back home, and everywhere."

Emma said, "All the land and sky and water—that's a lot to make!"

Brooke said, "And everything God made was very good."

God Made Sky, Water, and Land

Bible story based on Genesis 1:1–10; Psalms 65:6–7; 135:7; Amos 4:13

When God made the world, one of the first things He did was split the sky from the water. And then He made land—from rolling hills and high mountains to low valleys and farmlands, from swamps and marshes to grassy fields and prairies. God made the sky and the water and the land with just His words. Isn't that amazing?

Let's talk about what it means to be missionaries like the Parker family. They had an important job. Do you know what it was? To tell other people about God's love and about our Savior, Jesus. The Parker family had to travel a long way, all the way from home to another country called India. When the Parkers were on the airplane ride to India, they felt like they could see the whole world below them. Do you remember what they saw?

As a family, look at a map or globe of the world (find one in your home or online). Where are the areas of land (continents)? Where are the areas of water (oceans)? Where do you live on this globe? Find it together. Now find India. Look how far the Parker family had to travel by airplane to get there. The world is huge! God made places on earth we haven't ever seen before.

What We Learned about God: God made sky, water, and land.

Let's Pray: Dear God, we're amazed by Your awesome power. This world You made is huge. There are many places we haven't seen yet. Thank You for missionaries like the Parker family who tell others about You. And thank You for creating such a wonderful place for us to live until we go to heaven to be with You forever. Amen.

God saw all that he had made, and it was very good.
Genesis 1:31

God Made Plants for Our World

Bible story based on Genesis 1:11–12; 2:9

At the very beginning, God made the world. Only God can make all the plants for our world. God made soft green grass to walk on. And He made trees that give cool shade. God saw that the trees and grass were very good.

God made fruits and vegetables that would be good to eat too! Some grew on trees and bushes. And some grew in the ground. God saw that the fruits and vegetables were very good.

God wanted beautiful colors in His world, so He made flowers. Some were yellow; some were red; some were blue; some were purple. God saw that the flowers were very good.

God made grass, trees, fruits, vegetables, and flowers. And God knew that everything was very good.

The Nature Walk

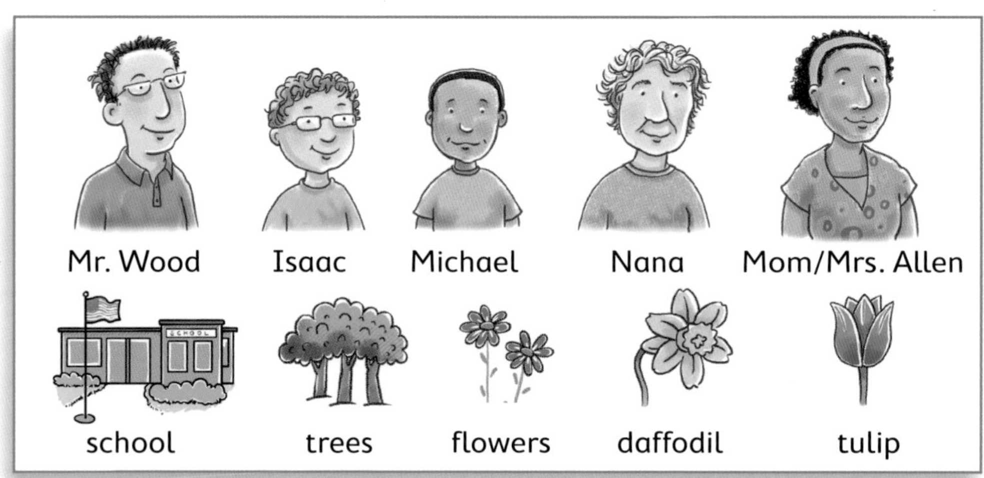

One day,  took his class on a nature walk around the . They saw  and . pointed to a flower and asked, "Do you know what this flower is?"

"I know! It's a ," said . "A  is 's favorite flower."

 and his class followed . They looked at the bright  and the leaves on the .

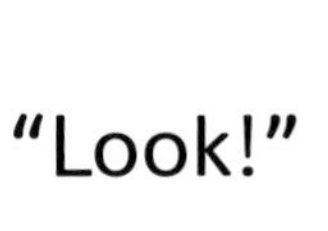

"Look!"  said. "Here is a . I helped my  plant some."

 helped each child cut a  or a  for the classroom.

After ,  told his  about the nature walk. "How do plants grow?" he asked.

"God makes plants grow from tiny seeds,"  said.

"Wow! God must be pretty amazing to make all of the different  and  we saw,"  said.

"Yes," agreed . "God is the only one who can make  and ."

Family Talk Time

God Made Plants for Our World

Bible story based on Genesis 1:11–12; 2:9

Only God can make a plant. We can put a seed into the ground or into a pot of soil, and if we water it and put it in the sunlight, we can watch it grow. But only God can make the seed. He knows exactly how to make the seed so it will grow into whatever He wants it to be. When God created the world, He put plants and trees into the ground. It was all part of His plan. The plants and trees are food for people and for animals.

Mr. Wood took his class for a walk outside the school. What did the children see? What did they take inside for their classroom?

You can do the activity at the back of the book to learn about some of the plants God created.

What We Learned about God: Only God can make plants.

Let's Pray: Dear God, Your creation is so beautiful. We can't begin to count all of the different types of flowers and trees and plants You have made. We know that only You can make these things. They give us shade from the sun and food to eat. And they even help make the air we breathe. Everything You do is perfect, Lord. Thank You for taking care of us. Amen.

Everything God created is good.
1 Timothy 4:4

God Made the Animals

Bible Story based on Genesis 1:20–25

1. God made all kinds of animals. He made the animals that live in the water. He made the birds that fly in the sky.

2. God made animals that live on the land, too. There are wild animals like striped zebras that run across the plains.

3. There are farm animals like cows that give us milk. And there are tiny worms that crawl under the ground.

4. God looked around the world. He saw that the animals had places to live and food to eat. God knew all the animals He made were very good.

The Newest Animal

Mr. Young brought Madison, Kaden, and their friends Alex and Sophia to Grandpa Young's farm to see the animals.

Grandpa was happy. He said, "I have a surprise. There is a new baby animal on the farm. Can you find it?" He gave them clues to find the newest animal. "The animal's legs are wobbly now," said Grandpa. "It will be able to stand better when it is older."

"Is it big?" asked Kaden.

"It's small now," said Grandpa. "But it will be big when it grows up."

Sophia and Madison looked around. *Cluck, cluck.* There was a mother chicken with baby chicks. Were the baby chicks the newest animals? Sophia remembered Grandpa Young said the newest animal would grow up to be big. The baby chicks would never be very big. They weren't the newest animal.

Alex and Kaden saw Pepper running around. *Ruff, ruff.* Pepper's legs weren't wobbly. Pepper wasn't the newest animal.

Sophia and Madison ran to the barn. *Neigh, neigh.* The girls saw Golden Boy, the pony. Golden Boy was old. He couldn't be the newest animal.

Then the girls heard Starlet the cow. *Moo, moo.*

Sophia grabbed Madison's arm. "Look," said Sophia. "Starlet has a baby!"

The girls watched the baby calf stand up. "Its legs are wobbly," said Madison. "And it keeps falling down."

Sophia said, "The calf is small. But it will be big like its mom someday."

"Kaden, Alex, we found it!" shouted the girls. The boys ran over to see the baby calf.

The baby calf went *moo, moo* in a little voice. It stayed safe and warm near its mother. The kids were happy to be at the farm to see the animals.

God Made the Animals

Bible story based on Genesis 1:20–25

This week we have been learning about the animals God created. From the beginning of time, God had a plan for the world and everything in it. Talk about the different types of fish, birds, and animals God created. What did He think of them?

Now think about the Young family farm. Do you remember what the newest baby animal on the farm was? What were some of the other animals the children found?

What are some animals you have seen in your own backyard or at a nearby park? Take turns sharing about your favorite animal, which God created. Why is it your favorite? Watch for your favorite animals this week (even if they are online). And when you see them, remember that God made them all!

What We Learned about God: God made the animals!

Let's Pray: Dear God, You are amazing. We thank You for all the animals You created. We know that everything You've made is very special, including us (name each family member, if you wish). Please help us take care of the world we live in. Amen.

How many are your works, LORD! In wisdom you made them all;
the earth is full of your creatures.
Psalm 104:24

God Made People

Bible Story based on Genesis 1:26–31; 2:7–8, 15, 18–23

God made a wonderful world. He made the land, sky, and water. God created the plants. He made all kinds of animals. Then God made a man. God named the man Adam. God put Adam in the garden of Eden to take care of the garden.

God told Adam to name the animals. So Adam did.

Adam needed a helper, so God made a woman and brought her to Adam. Adam named the woman Eve. Eve helped Adam take care of the world that God made. Adam and Eve took care of the plants by helping them grow. They cared for the animals by being kind to them. God wants people to care for His world.

Farm Chores

Kaden was visiting Grandpa's farm again, this time with his friend Michael. Kaden showed Michael around the farm.

Grandpa Young walked past the boys, carrying a pail of water. "I'm glad I found you," he said. "I need some help. Grandma usually helps me, but she's busy making dinner."

"Wow!" said Michael. "I've never worked on a farm before."

"Let's feed Golden Boy first," said Grandpa. "Then you can brush his coat and get all the dirt out of it. He loves being brushed."

It took a long time to brush out Golden Boy's coat. When the boys were done, Golden Boy pranced around and neighed.

"That's his way of saying thank-you," said Kaden.

"Now what can we do?" asked Michael.

"We could feed Grandpa's dog, Pepper," said Kaden. So the boys put a scoop of dog food in Pepper's bowl. Pepper ate all his food. Then he wagged his tail.

"Look, he's thanking us," said Michael.

Then the boys saw the rabbit cage. The rabbits were hungry, and their cage needed to be cleaned. "I know how to take care of rabbits," said Michael. "Munchkin is my pet rabbit at home."

The boys put fresh paper in the rabbits' cage. Then they fed the rabbits some hay and green vegetables. The rabbits' noses twitched as they nibbled on their food, almost as if they were smiling.

Clang, clang. "What's that loud noise?" asked Michael. "It sounds like a big bell."

"That's Grandma's way of letting us know it's dinnertime," said Kaden.

"We helped your grandpa take care of the animals," said Michael. "Now your grandma is taking care of us! Let's go. I'm hungry!"

God Made People

Bible story based on Genesis 1:26–31; 2:7–8, 15, 18–23

After God made the world—night and day, land and water, plants and animals—He made people to live in it. Do you remember the name of the very first man? And what was the name of the very first woman? People were God's most special creation. Adam and Eve lived in the garden of Eden. God had made this special place just for them. And He gave them a very important job. What was it?

Back at the Young family farm, Kaden and his friend Michael helped with the chores. Name some of the ways they helped Grandpa Young. They did a great job helping!

Did you know that we still have this same job as Adam and Eve—to take care of God's beautiful world? There are many ways we can do this together. Consider putting up a bird feeder or birdhouse at home. Or if you'd like an indoor pet, consider adopting one from a local animal shelter. You could also visit the zoo as a family and discover all the amazing animals God created.

What We Learned about God: God wants people to care for His world.

Let's Pray: Dear God, You have given us a beautiful world to live in. Help us remember the job You gave us—to take care of it. We love You, Lord. Amen.

So God created mankind in his own image, in the image of God he created them; male and female he created them.
Genesis 1:27

God Keeps Noah Safe

Bible story based on Genesis 6:5–22; 7:11–17, 24

1. Noah loved God, and God loved Noah. God told Noah, "There will be a flood." Then God said to build a big boat called an ark.

2. Noah got the wood to build the ark. He sawed the wood, and he hammered the pieces together, then he filled all of the cracks.

3. Next God told Noah to put two of every kind of animal on the ark. So he did. Then Noah and his family got on the ark, and God closed the door.

4. It rained so hard that the whole earth was covered with water. But God kept Noah and his family and the animals safe.

A Trip to the Zoo

Sophia and her mom were going to have a special day together. They decided to go to the zoo because Sophia loved to see all the different animals.

When they got to the zoo, Sophia ran ahead. Mrs. Lopez called out, "Sophia, stop! Stay with me!"

Mrs. Lopez ran after Sophia and caught up to her. "Sophia, we have all day to see the animals. I want to help keep you safe. Please stay with me."

Sophia said, "I'm sorry, Mama."

Sophia wanted to see the penguins first. They watched the penguins splash in the water. They even got to watch a zookeeper feed fish to the penguins.

Then Sophia and her mom walked hand in hand to see the giraffes. Ms. Lopez bought Sophia some crackers so they could feed the giraffes. Sophia held the crackers as a giraffe stuck out its long purple tongue to take one.

"Mama!" Sophia squealed as she pulled her hand away. "His tongue is all rough. It feels like sandpaper." Mrs. Lopez told her that God made giraffes that way. When the crackers were gone, Sophia skipped off to see the tigers. Mrs. Lopez was right behind her.

There they discovered a surprise. One of the tigers had a new cub! Sophia pressed against the glass and said, "Oh, Mama, I wish I could hold the baby cub!"

Ms. Lopez replied, "Sophia, that cub is cute, but it's still a wild animal. The tall glass is needed. It keeps the animals safe in their area and us safe from the animals."

As they left the zoo, Sophia thought for a minute, then said, "I'm glad you keep me safe, Mama. I'm glad God keeps us safe too."

God Keeps Noah Safe

Bible story based on Genesis 6:5–22; 7:11–17, 24

God protected Noah and the animals from the flood in the Bible story. What did God ask Noah to make? How many of each type of animal went into the ark?

When Sophia and her mom went to the zoo, they saw many different types of animals. Do you remember what some of them were? The tiger cub must have looked really cute, almost like a kitten. Why was it important that the glass was between the tigers and the zoo visitors?

In your own family, what are some things that keep you safe? Some examples are seat belts, bike helmets, and looking both ways before crossing a street. Sometimes you may have forgotten to stay safe. Share what happened.

What We Learned about God: God cares about our safety.

Let's Pray: Dear God, thank You for taking care of us and everything You have made, including the animals. Animals are such a special part of Your creation, Lord. Help us be like You and take care of them. Please keep us safe as we go about all of the things we do. Help us remember ways to stay safe. Amen.

You are my hiding place; you will protect me from trouble.
Psalm 32:7

God's Plan for Abram

Bible story based on Genesis 12:1–9

1. God planned for Abram to move to a new land. So Abram and his wife, Sarai, and his nephew, Lot, packed all of their things.

2. Abram obeyed God's plan. God showed Abram the way to his new land.

3. After many days Abram and his family came to the land God was giving to them. They knew God's plan was very good.

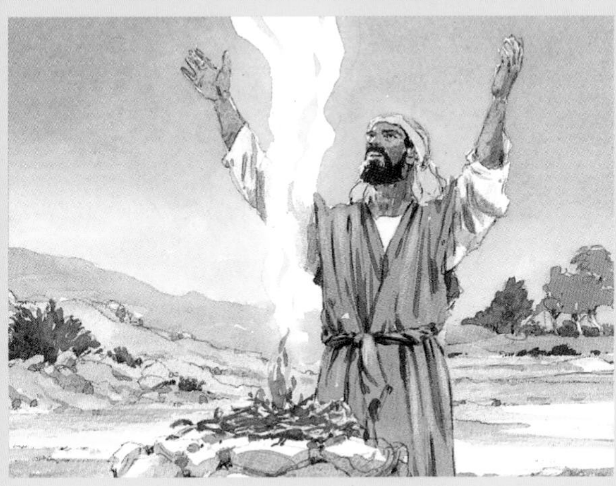

4. Abram thanked God for showing him His plan.

A Big Plan

Mr. Young had a surprise for his Sunday school class. "Someone is coming today to tell us a story. His story is about following God to a new land." No one could guess who was coming.

Then Dr. Li walked into the room. He was carrying a large globe. A globe is a map of the world in the shape of a ball. "I have a special story to tell you," began Dr. Li. "It started many years ago in a faraway country called China."

Kaden raised his hand and asked, "Where is China?"

"China is a very large country," said Dr. Li. "It's far away on the other side of the Pacific Ocean." Dr. Li pointed to China on the globe. He also pointed to where they lived.

"Mrs. Li and I used to live in China. But I felt God wanted me to become a doctor," said Dr. Li. "Mrs. Li and I prayed. We asked God if His plan was for me to be a doctor. We listened to God. In many ways we knew God was saying, 'Yes, I want you to be a doctor.'

"There wasn't a school for doctors near our home in China, so we asked God where He planned for me to learn to be a doctor. When I talked to other people about learning to be a doctor, they told me to go to America."

Dr. Li continued. "Mrs. Li and I prayed. We listened to God. God helped us know His plan for us to move to America so I could go to a school for doctors."

"How did you get here?" asked Isaac. "China is so far away."

Dr. Li smiled. "We saved our money. Then we packed most of our things in a very big box. That box came on a boat to America. Mrs. Li and I both had a suitcase with the things we would need until the boat arrived in America. We flew here in a plane. The big box was sent to the place where we lived while I was learning to be a doctor."

"Evan was born while I was in school to be a doctor," said Dr. Li. "After I became a doctor, we moved here.

"We know we're doing what God wants us to do. But we still ask God about His plan for us. We're still listening to God for what He plans next."

God's Plan for Abram

Bible story based on Genesis 12:1–9

Talk together about the plan God had for Abram in the Bible story. What did God ask Abram to do? How did Abram respond to what God asked him to do?

In Mr. Young's Sunday school class, who came to visit? What did Dr. and Mrs. Li do as a way to find out God's plan for Dr. Li to become a doctor? And then where did they go?

Talk about the ways your family can learn about God's plan for you. Spending time with God is very important. We can spend time with God by learning about the Bible and by praying. Take time during the week to pray about God's plan for your family.

What We Learned about God: God has a plan for us.

Let's Pray: Dear Lord, we know that You have a plan for each one of us and that You also have a plan for our family. Help us follow wherever You lead us. Thank You for the gift of prayer, because through prayer, we can talk with You. We know that You always hear us when we pray. Help us also listen to what You are saying to us. Amen.

Trust in the LORD with all your heart.
Proverbs 3:5

God Keeps His Promise

Bible story based on Genesis 15:1–6; 21:1–6

1. One night Abram was praying and listening to God. Abram said, "Lord, I have everything I need. All I want is children of my own."

2. God said, "I will give you a son." He said, "Count the stars if you can. You will have that many people in your family someday."

3. Abram started to count the stars. There were too many to count! God had promised Abram a big family.

4. God kept His promise. Abram and Sarai had a son, Isaac. God also gave them new names: Abraham and Sarah.

Where's Lunch?

 and  were playing with  in her backyard. "I'll bring  when it's time," said .

, , and  played on the .

After a long time,  said, "It must be time for . I'm hungry."

 said, "Me, too. Where's ?"

 said, "  said she would bring us ."

 said, "She wouldn't forget."

"It must not be time yet," said . "Let's play."

So they played on the .

"I'm really hungry now!" said .

 saw  bringing a tray with . They all ran to the table.

 said, "You must be hungry. Some days it's hard to wait for ."

 just smiled.

God Keeps His Promise

Bible story based on Genesis 15:1–6; 21:1–6

In the Bible story, Abram had everything he needed except for one thing. What was it, do you remember? What do the stars have to do with God's promise to Abram? What new names did God give to Abram and Sarai?

When Michael and Sophia were playing at Mia's house, what were they waiting for? Who was supposed to bring it to them? Did she keep her promise?

As a family, think about promises. Doesn't it feel great when someone keeps a promise? We know we can always count on God to keep His promises. Can we count on each other as a family? Talk about this together. Are there some examples of how you have kept your promises to each other? What about times when promises were not kept? Why is it important to keep a promise?

What We Learned about God: God always keeps His promises.

Let's Pray: Dear God our Father, thank You for who You are. We know that You keep every single promise You make. And we know we can put our trust in You no matter what. Please help us keep our promises to each other as a family and also with our friends. Help us be more like You as much as we can. Lord, there will be times when we break our promises to each other. Help us have forgiving hearts toward each other. And help us remember that each day is a new beginning. Amen.

I will surely bless you.
Hebrews 6:14

Esau and Jacob Are Different

Bible story based on Genesis 25:20–28

1. Isaac and Rebekah had twin baby boys. They named the babies Jacob and Esau. Both babies needed to be fed and rocked and loved.

2. But in some ways the babies were different. Esau had a lot of red hair. Jacob had less hair, and it wasn't red.

3. When the brothers grew up, Esau liked to hunt for food and be out in the forest. Jacob liked to be near the tents and help with the fires and cooking.

4. God made Jacob and Esau. They were the same age. They were alike in some ways and different in others. God made each of us different.

Family Pictures

Mr. Young brought some special pictures to Sunday school one day. Mrs. Li had taken the pictures during the week.

After the children learned how Jacob and Esau were different during the Bible story, Mr. Young put the pictures on the table for everyone to see. He asked the children to find the picture of their own family.

Michael found his picture first. "I'm the only child in my family," he said. "God gave me dark hair and eyes like my dad and mom."

Isaac looked at his picture. "There's my brother. I have glasses and Caleb doesn't," Isaac said.

Madison and Kaden laughed when they saw their picture. "Kaden and I have the same color hair and eyes because we're twins," said Madison.

"But Chloe has brown hair like our mom," Kaden added. "I'm glad God made us different."

Sophia looked carefully at the picture of her family. "I have a brother," she said. "I'm bigger than Alex. But my mom said he'll be taller than me when he grows up."

Mia smiled when she saw her family together. "I look different from my brother because I'm adopted," said Mia. "We all love each other very much."

Evan looked at the last picture. "God gave me a little sister," he said. "We both have brown eyes!"

The children looked at all of the pictures. Some children were tall and some were short. They had different colors of hair, skin, and eyes.

Madison said, "We all look different except for one thing. God gave each of us a big, happy smile!"

Esau and Jacob Are Different

Bible story based on Genesis 25:20–28

God made each of us different. Look at pictures of Jacob and Esau in the Bible story. What is different about them? What is the same? Are they related to each other? Yes, they're twin brothers, even though they look so different from each other.

Now let's talk about the children who were in Sunday school. Do you remember what some of the differences were between them? What did they all have that was the same? Yes, a big, happy smile!

Has anyone ever told you that you look like your brother or sister or cousin? Usually people in a family look similar. Look at each other. What is the same? What is different? Even if you see some things that are the same, God made each of us different from each other. This includes what we're interested in doing—our hobbies and activities. Talk about some of these things together. Take turns sharing what each person in your family enjoys and how each of you is different from one another.

What We Learned about God: God made each of us different.

Let's Pray: Dear God, thank You for making each of us different from each other. Sometimes it can be hard when people don't like the things we do, but help us use these times as a way to learn how to accept and understand others. You have made our family and friends and everyone in the whole world as individual, special creations. Help us appreciate that and learn from it. Amen.

I praise you because I am fearfully and wonderfully made.
Psalm 139:14

Jacob Worships God

Bible story based on Genesis 28:10–22

1. Jacob was on a long trip. All day he walked and walked. When the sun went down, Jacob was very tired.

2. Jacob put his head on a rock and slept. He dreamed about angels on a stairway to heaven. God said, "I will always be with you wherever you go."

3. Jacob woke up. He said, "I know God is with me wherever I go. And I want people to know that this is a special place to worship God."

4. In the morning Jacob took his stone pillow and made a special place to worship God. Jacob started on his trip again. He knew God was with him.

A Long Trip Home

The Young family was driving home from vacation. They had visited some mountains. Their vacation had been fun, but the drive home was not fun at all. For miles and miles, they drove over flat land with nothing to see but cows and row after row of corn.

Kaden had listened to all of his CDs. Madison had read all of her picture books. They had both eaten too many raisins and crackers.

"How much longer?" asked Madison.

Mom sighed. She was ready to get home too. "A few more hours," she said.

"How about some music?" asked Dad. "That will help the time go faster."

"But I'm tired of the CDs we brought," said Kaden.

"I know!" Madison said excitedly. "Let's make up our own songs! Let's sing the song we sang when we were on the top of the mountain."

Madison sang the song to the tune of "Mary Had a Little Lamb."

God is on the mountaintop,
mountaintop, mountaintop.
God is on the mountaintop.
He's with us where we go!

"But, Madison, we can't sing that song! We're not on the mountaintop anymore," said Kaden.

"You're right, Kaden," said Dad. "Let's sing it about a long, flat road. God is with us here, too." So they sang about the long, flat road.

God is on the long, flat road;
long, flat road; long, flat road.
God is on the long, flat road.
He's with us where we go!

Madison and Kaden sang and sang. Soon they weren't on the long, flat road anymore. So they sang, "God is on the silver bridge," and "God is by the grocery store." But the best verse of all was when they finally sang, "God is with us at our house. He's with us where we go!" Even Chloe sang that verse!

Family Talk Time

Jacob Worships God

Bible story based on Genesis 28:10–22

God made an important promise to Jacob in the Bible story. Do you remember what it was? God promised to always be with Jacob. God promises to always be with us as well.

Coming back from vacation, the Young family sang a song. Do you remember what it was about? Where is God?

Talk about the coming week and all the places you will go. Will God be with you? In the car? At school? At home? At church? At the grocery store? How can He do that? Share what you think and feel about this.

What We Learned about God: God is with us wherever we go.

Let's Pray: Dear God, thank You for Your promise to always be with us. During our busy days, we go to many different places. And we know that You are with us wherever we are, including right here at home. Please be with each of us this week, Lord. Help us to learn and grow and then come back home safely each day. Amen.

And so we know and rely on the love God has for us. God is love. Whoever lives in love lives in God, and God in them.
1 John 4:16

Joseph Forgives His Brothers

Bible story based on Genesis 37:27–28; 45:1–15

1. Joseph's brothers didn't like him. They sold him to people who took Joseph to Egypt to be a slave.

2. After Joseph grew up, he worked for the pharaoh of Egypt. Joseph sold food to the people.

3. One day Joseph's brothers came to buy food. They didn't recognize Joseph. When he told them who he was, they were afraid of him.

4. But Joseph said, "Don't be afraid. I forgive you for being mean to me."

Where's Slowpoke?

 put in his .

"Can't we still play with him?" asked .

 said, "He needs to rest. I'll get his lunch." When  went into the ,  took out of the . "How fast can you go?"  asked.  walked past a .

came out of the  with 's food.

"I'll put  back," thought . He looked, but he didn't see .

"Where's ?"  asked when he saw the empty .

"I let him out to play," said . "Now he's gone. Let's look together."

 and  looked by the . They looked under the . "Here he is!"  said.

 got  and put him back in his .

"I'm sorry I let  out," said .

"I forgive you,"  told him.

Joseph Forgives His Brothers

Bible story based on Genesis 37:27–28; 45:1–15

Joseph had a problem in this Bible story. Do you remember what it was? Where did he have to go? When Joseph saw his brothers again, what important decision did he make? Do you think it was easy or hard for him to forgive his brothers like that?

What kind of pet did Alex have? When Alex went inside, what did Kaden do? Where did they eventually find Slowpoke? What important decision did Alex have to make? Do you think it was easy or hard for Alex to forgive Kaden? Why or why not?

Now, as a family, talk about forgiveness. Does someone want to share a time when he or she forgave someone (another family member, friend, or someone else)? Was it easy or hard? How did it feel after forgiving the person? Now talk about how wonderful it is that God forgives us. When we make mistakes—and everyone does—we can go to God and tell Him we're sorry. He will forgive us.

What We Learned about God: God's Word tells us to forgive others when they hurt us.

Let's Pray: Dear God, sometimes it's hard to remember that we all make mistakes. Please help us forgive other people. Help us try to be like You, Lord, and give people second chances through forgiveness. It's hard to do this, but please make us strong so that we can get past the wrong things people do and give them another chance. Thank You for forgiving our sins. May we always remember how important it is to forgive. Amen.

Be kind and compassionate to one another, forgiving each other, just as in Christ God forgave you.
Ephesians 4:32

Miriam Helps Her Baby Brother

Bible story based on Exodus 1:6–2:10

1. Miriam was watching her baby brother, Moses. He was in a basket floating on a river. His family had hidden him there so the king of Egypt wouldn't find him.

2. Miriam saw the princess come to the river. The princess found baby Moses and felt sorry for him.

3. Miriam ran to the princess and asked, "Shall I get someone to help take care of the baby?" The princess agreed.

4. Miriam brought her mother to the river. The princess gave baby Moses to his mother to take care of him. Moses would be safe now.

A Day at the Park

"Why does Chloe have to go with me to the park?" asked Kaden.

"Chloe is older. She can watch you," said Dad.

Mom hugged Kaden. "We love you. We want you to be safe," she said.

Chloe and Kaden walked to the park. Kaden saw a squirrel and ran after it.

He climbed a fence to see better. His shirt got caught. "Help! I can't get down," he cried. Chloe helped. Kaden said, "Thanks!" He jumped down and ran ahead.

“See how fast I can run!” he said. Chloe ran with Kaden all the way to the park. Then Kaden started to swing across the rings. “Look at me,” he yelled. “Help! I’m falling!” Kaden shouted. Chloe helped Kaden finish the rings.

Chloe pushed Kaden on the swing. When he fell, she helped him up. She tied his shoes. When he jumped in a puddle, Chloe cleaned the mud off Kaden’s shoes.

At home, Dad asked, “Did you have fun?”

“Yes,” Kaden said. “I followed a squirrel. We ran to the park. I played on the rings. Chloe pushed me on the swings. I jumped in a mud puddle. Chloe helped me all the time. I’m glad she’s my sister.”

Chloe was glad Kaden was part of her family too.

Miriam Helps Her Baby Brother

Bible story based on Exodus 1:6–2:10

In the Bible story, do you remember how God saved Moses? Why was Moses in a basket? God helps families care for each other. Even when it seems impossible, God can make a way!

When Kaden and his sister Chloe went to the park together, what were some of the things Kaden did? How did Chloe help him? Why do you think she helped him? What do you think might have happened to Kaden if Chloe hadn't been with him?

In your family, you help each other. Why? Because you care about each other. Think over the past week. Share some of the ways your family showed that you care about each other. For example, did someone help with homework, give someone else a ride, cheer on a family member at a game, make supper, or perhaps pray for someone else? God works through other people to care for us, especially families.

What We Learned about God: God wants people in families to care for one another.

Let's Pray: Dear God, thank You for our family. Families are very special. Help us show that we care about each other. Help us remember that You want us to do this. We can always learn how to do this better through reading the Bible and all the examples You show us there. Amen.

Let us love one another, for love comes from God.
1 John 4:7

God Helps His People

Bible story based on Exodus 14:1–31

God's people were slaves of the pharaoh of Egypt. Moses led the Israelites out of Egypt.

The people left Egypt with all they owned. Then they stopped traveling to camp by a sea.

Pharaoh and his army came to bring the Israelites back to Egypt. The Israelites were afraid! They asked God to help.

Moses held his arms out over the sea. God made a strong wind split the sea.

Now the people could walk through on dry land.

When the people were on the other side, God let the wind stop. The water crashed over Pharaoh's army.

God helped His people when they were afraid!

Afraid!

Mia, please put away your toys and get ready for bed.
... In Jesus's name. Amen.
Good night, Mia. I love you.
Daddy, don't turn out the light. I don't like the dark.
I'll turn on your nightlight. Don't forget your Bible verse. Let's say it together.
When I am afraid, I will trust in You.
Good night, Mia.
DADDY!

What's wrong?
The storm woke me up. I'm scared.

Mia, remember God is always with you and can help you when you're scared. Let's say your Bible verse together.
When I am afraid, I will trust in You.

Sometimes I forget God can help me when I am scared. Will you stay here for a little bit while I fall asleep again?
Sure, Mia. Let's pray and ask God to help you not be afraid of the storm and to get back to sleep quickly.

Family Talk Time

God Helps His People

Bible story based on Exodus 14:1–31

In the Bible story, when God's people were in Egypt, they were slaves. Who led them out of Egypt? Who chased after them? What did God do to the sea? After God's people went through, what happened to the sea?

When it was time for bed, Mia asked her dad to keep something on. What was it? Why did she want it on? Then what happened outside? What did Mia's dad remind her about God?

Sometimes we are afraid, like Mia. Together as a family, talk about what types of things make you feel afraid. What calms you down when you're afraid? Sometimes it's easy to forget to pray. But it will help. God always knows what is happening. He wants us to talk with Him as much as we can. Consider making a special pillowcase that you can keep in the linen closet. Write this reminder on it with a permanent marker: God is with me. Whenever someone in your family is afraid, pull out this pillowcase and slip it over the person's pillow. Or consider leaving your family Bible open on the kitchen table to a scripture that can help. Take turns finding other scriptures you can turn to when you are in the kitchen throughout the day or week.

What We Learned about God: God can help us when we're afraid.

Let's Pray: Dear God, we need to remember that You are always with us and that You know everything that's happening in our lives. You understand us even better than our own family. Please help us remember to pray to You, like we're doing right now, as much as we can, including when we are afraid. Help us find ways to help each other when we are afraid. And may we remember to give You our fears and worries. You will help carry us through. Thank You, Lord. Amen.

When I am afraid, I put my trust in you.
Psalm 56:3

God Gives His People Food

Bible story based on Exodus 16:11–18

1. Moses and the Israelites were traveling to their new land. They had been walking through the desert for weeks.

2. The people didn't have any more food. They complained, "Moses, we need food to eat!" God told Moses that He would take care of the people.

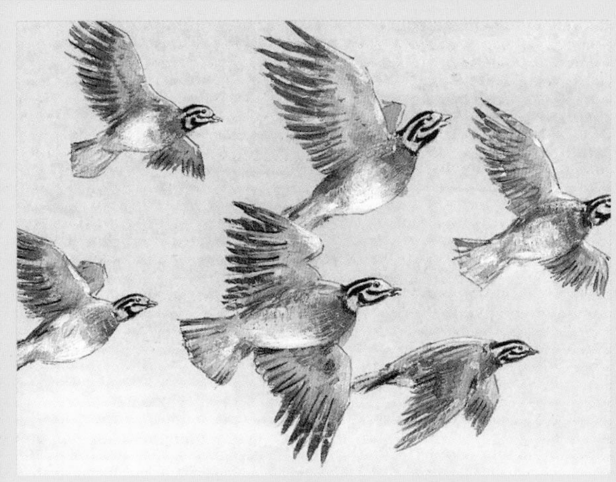

3. That night God sent a flock of quail to the people. God gave the people meat.

4. The next morning the people saw white stuff on the ground. Moses told them, "It's manna—bread from God." And everyone ate!

Carrots!

Evan and Kaden were helping Mrs. Li by putting away groceries. Ava was helping too.

Ava picked up a bunch of carrots. "Where do these come from?"

Kaden and Evan looked at each other. "They come from the grocery store. Mom bought them," said Evan.

Kaden added, "The store gets the carrots from farmers. They grow carrots in big gardens. That's where they *really* come from."

Kaden was going to visit Grandpa Young's farm the next day. He invited Evan and Ava to go with him.

At the farm Kaden asked, "Grandpa, will you please show us your garden?"

"Let's go!" said Grandpa Young. He led the children to his big garden. There were rows and rows of tomatoes. There were rows and rows of beans. There were rows and rows of onions. And there were rows and rows of carrots. He showed the children how to pull up the carrots and onions.

Ava pulled up a carrot and asked, "How did this get in the ground?"

Kaden's grandpa showed Ava some tiny carrot seeds. He showed her how to put the seeds in the ground. He told her, "God sends the sun and rain to help the seeds grow."

Kaden said, "The tiny seeds grow green tops and orange carrot bottoms. When the carrots are big enough, they are pulled from the ground. Then Grandpa sells them to the grocery store."

"You can buy carrots at the store, Ava," said Grandpa Young. "But it's God who sends the sun and rain for the seeds to grow. So it's really God who gives us carrots."

God Gives His People Food

Bible story based on Exodus 16:11–18

After God's people crossed through the Red Sea, where did they have to go next? What was the problem? What were the two different types of food God gave His people? Did you know that God fed His people this way in the dessert for forty years? That's a long time!

Who were Evan and Kaden and Ava helping with the groceries? Where did the carrots come from? Where did the children go the following day? What did they see? Who makes gardens grow?

As a family, go into the kitchen and open your refrigerator. Choose an item and describe how it was made. Then think about how God really made everything in your refrigerator, because He made animals and sun and rain and soil and everything that is needed in order to make food. Now choose a favorite item and explain why you like it so much. If you have permission, go ahead and have a little snack!

What We Learned about God: God gives us food.

Let's Pray: Dear God, we are so thankful for the food You provide for us. Without You, there wouldn't be anything in our refrigerator, and there wouldn't be any food for anyone to eat. Help us remember that all things come from You. Please show us ways we can help others who don't have enough to eat. We know You want us to help each other. Amen.

Give us today our daily bread.
Matthew 6:11

God Gives His People Water

Bible story based on Exodus 17:1–6

Moses and the Israelites camped in the desert. It was hot and dry, and they couldn't find water.

The people complained to Moses, "Give us water to drink!"

Moses asked God what to do. God told Moses what to do. Moses went to a large rock. *Whack*! Moses hit the rock with his staff. *Whoosh*! God made water gush out of the rock.

The people came and drank so they were no longer thirsty. God took care of His people by giving them water.

A Very Hot Day

I don't know who lives there.
Look! The firefighters are spraying water on the house. I hope they have enough water.
I hope the people who live there are okay.

Thank God everything is fine. We had enough water to put out the fire. and no one was hurt. It's so hot out, you kids should run through the sprinkler!
Yes, let's do that!

God Gives His People Water

Bible story based on Exodus 17:1–6

In the Bible story, God's people were in the middle of the desert. They were very, very thirsty, and they really needed water. How did God give His people water? What did God tell Moses to do?

On a hot summer day, what happened in the children's neighborhood? Have you ever seen firefighters put out a fire? What are some tools or equipment they need in order to put out fires? What's the most important thing they need? Yes, it's water.

Talk about the different things you need water for in your house, including water for any pets or plants or even dishes. Where does water come from? Can anyone make water? Only God can make water. It's a precious gift He gives to us, and we need it every single day in order to live.

What We Learned about God: God gives us water, which we need to survive!

Let's Pray: Dear God, You give us so many important things we need in order to live, including water. We need it for so many things, Lord. Help us be responsible and not waste water, but to be thankful for it. Amen.

For he satisfies the thirsty and fills the hungry with good things.
Psalm 107:9

God Gives Us Rules

Bible story based on Exodus 19:1–25; 20:1–17

The Israelites camped by Mount Sinai. God told Moses to climb the mountain. God gave Moses rules for all God's people. The first rule was to love God. This means God's people must love God more than anything or anyone else. Another rule was to worship God. God's people were to keep one day each week to show their love for God.

The next rule was to honor one's father and mother. This means God's people had to listen to and obey their parents. God wanted them to be polite and respectful toward their moms and dads.

Two rules were short: do not steal; do not lie. It's wrong to take things that belong to others, and God's people should always tell the truth.

Two other rules were given too: do not misuse the name of the LORD and do not murder.

God wrote the ten most important rules on stone tablets. They are also in the Bible for us to read. They are called the Ten Commandments.

Rules of the Game

On Saturday afternoon, Isaac and Caleb Mitchell lay on the floor of the living room playing their favorite board game.

"Three, four, five," Isaac counted as he moved his game piece and landed in the mud pit.

Caleb rolled, counted out three, and picked up a treasure card. Isaac rolled again and moved ahead two spaces.

"Isaac, that's not how you play!" shouted Caleb. "You landed on the mud pit. Now you have to be stuck until you get a six. You only got a two."

"It's too hard that way. I'll never get a six. You're already winning. It doesn't matter. I'm changing the rules," said Isaac.

"You can't change the rules," Caleb said.

"You change the rules all the time. How come I can't do it?" Isaac asked.

"I do not!" Caleb argued.

Mr. Mitchell heard the boys arguing and walked into the room. "Boys, what's going on in here?" he asked.

"Isaac is trying to cheat so he doesn't have to stay in the mud pit," Caleb said with a grumpy face.

"No, I'm not!" Isaac yelled. "The rules are too hard and Caleb is going to win."

The boys' dad sat down next to them and said, "We all like to change the rules, especially when it will help us. But God gives us rules for a reason. Rules keep us safe and help us get along with others."

Caleb looked at Isaac and asked, "Are you ready to play fair?"

"Yes, but I better roll a six this time," said Isaac, smiling.

Family Talk Time

God Gives Us Rules

Bible story based on Exodus 19:1–25; 20:1–17

In the Bible story, God called Moses to go up a mountain to meet with Him. What did God give to Moses? What were God's rules written on? Do we still need to follow these rules today?

When Isaac and Caleb were playing a game, what went wrong? What does "playing fair" mean? Who helped the boys figure out what the right thing to do was?

Be honest with each other and name some rules that are hard for you to follow. Explain why. Now read through the Ten Commandments, found in Exodus 20. Count how many times God says "You shall not." Does that mean we can break rules when we feel like it? We aren't perfect, but we do need to do our best to follow what is right.

What We Learned about God: God gives us rules.

Let's Pray: Dear God, thank You for giving us rules to follow. You know that we need them in order to figure out what is right and what is wrong. Sometimes we don't follow the rules, because we aren't perfect. Please help us do better. And thank You for sending Jesus to be our Savior, because He *did* follow all of the rules. Help us try to be more like Jesus. Amen.

Give me understanding, so that I may keep your law
and obey it with all my heart.
Psalm 119:34

Ruth and Naomi

Bible story based on Ruth 1–4

1. Ruth lived with Naomi, who was like a mother to her. Ruth loved Naomi and stayed with Naomi to help her.

2. Naomi and Ruth were poor so they couldn't buy food. Ruth went to a field to pick up leftover grain they could eat.

3. Boaz was the owner of the field. Boaz was very kind to Ruth. He let her pick up as much grain as she needed.

4. Ruth took the grain home so she could make bread for herself and Naomi. God was pleased with the way Ruth showed her love for Naomi.

Saturday with Nana

Isaac liked Saturdays. His dad always made snowman pancakes for breakfast.

One Saturday, Mr. Mitchell was taking Isaac's brother, Caleb, camping. Nana would take care of Isaac. Isaac loved Nana, but Saturday wouldn't be the same without pancakes.

When Nana came on Friday, Isaac took her suitcase to her room. "Thank you, Isaac," said Nana. "You're a good helper."

Nana and Isaac made ants-on-a-log. Nana spread the peanut butter on celery sticks. Isaac put on the raisins. "You sure are a good helper," Nana said with a smile.

Nana and Isaac played three games of checkers. Checkers was Nana's favorite game.

"Time for bed," said Nana.

Isaac wasn't ready to go to bed. But he obeyed anyway.

Saturday morning, Isaac didn't smell pancakes. Nana hadn't made any breakfast. Nana said, "Isaac, you have been such a good helper. Let's go out for breakfast!"

Isaac and Nana went to the Pancake Patch. Isaac got pancakes. What a fun time he had with Nana!

Ruth and Naomi

Bible story based on Ruth 1–4

In the Bible story, Naomi's husband and her grown-up sons had died. Ruth had been married to one of Naomi's sons. Ruth decided to stay with Naomi. She loved Naomi and wanted to help her. And then amazing things started to happen. Who was Boaz? What did he let Ruth gather for food? Guess what. Ruth and Boaz got married. They took good care of Naomi and had a little baby boy named Obed.

At the Mitchells' house, why did Isaac like Saturdays so much? Who visited Isaac? What were some of the things Nana and Isaac did together? And what about the pancakes? Where did they eat them? What did Nana tell Isaac? Yes, that he was a good helper.

As a family, what are some ways you help each other? Take turns sharing a few of these ways. Why do you help each other? Because it shows our love for each other. We don't need to follow a list, but we should be ready to help when we see it's needed. What are some ways you can help each other? Talk about them together.

What We Learned about God: God wants us to love our families.

Let's Pray: Dear God, thank You for our family. Help us show our love for each other by helping each other. Even when we're busy, help us remember that our family is very important and that we must put each other in front of other things. Please open up ways we can help others around us—neighbors, friends, people at church, whomever You decide. Amen.

And now these three remain: faith, hope and love.
But the greatest of these is love.
1 Corinthians 13:13

Solomon Pleases God

Bible story based on 1 Kings 3:1–15

Solomon was the king of Israel after his father, David, died. Solomon showed his love for God by making good choices. One night God talked to Solomon while he was sleeping. God said, "Solomon, ask for anything you want Me to give you."

Some people would have asked for lots of money. But not Solomon. Solomon said, "Lord, it's scary being the king of so many people. Please help me to make wise choices for Your people."

God was pleased about what Solomon asked for. So God made Solomon wise. God also made Solomon rich and let him live a long time. As long as Solomon asked for God's help, he pleased God with his choices.

The Right Choice

I think they should stay in the tent.
No, I think they should build another wood church.

I think we should pray for them to make the right choice. Let's pray for them right now.

Dear Jesus, thank You for keeping our friends safe. Please help them make the right choice to either rebuild the wood church or to stay in the tent. In Jesus's name. Amen.

Solomon Pleases God

Bible story based on 1 Kings 3:1–15

In the Bible story, King Solomon was fast asleep. What did he ask God for? Was God pleased about what the king asked for? How did God bless King Solomon?

Remember the Parker family? In what country were they missionaries? What happened to their church? What was the decision they were trying to make?

Every single day, we make many decisions. Just think about your day so far. What decisions have you already made? Making decisions is a normal part of every single day. Sometimes we make good choices, and sometimes we make bad choices. What can happen when we make a bad choice? Talk about this together. What happens when we make a good choice? One choice leads to another, and that's why it's so important to make good choices.

What We Learned about God: Making good choices pleases God.

Let's Pray: Dear God, thank You for allowing us to make decisions. Help us think very carefully about the choices we make. Please lead us to make good choices by asking for Your help. We want to honor You with our good choices. Please forgive us for the bad choices we've made. Help us learn from the times we've made mistakes. Amen.

Love the Lord your God with all your heart
and with all your soul and with all your mind.
Matthew 22:37

A Widow Shares What She Has

Bible story based on 1 Kings 17:8–16

1. Elijah was a prophet of God. He was very hungry and asked a woman for food. The woman looked sad. She said, "I have only a little flour and oil."

2. Elijah told her to make him some bread. Elijah said, "Don't worry. Share what you have. God will give you oil and flour."

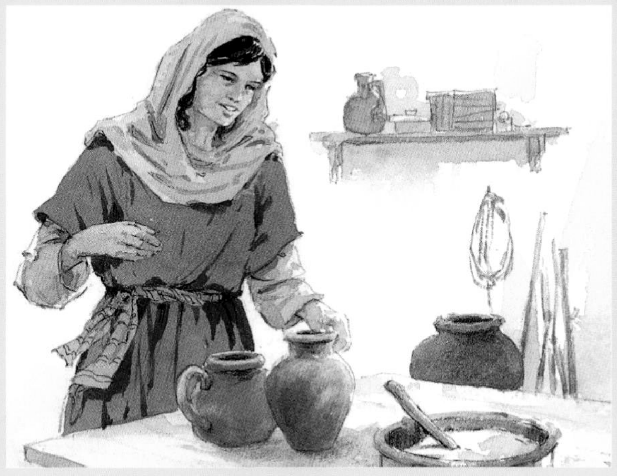

3. The woman baked bread for Elijah. Then God put more oil in her jug and more flour in her jar.

4. The woman was then able to make bread for her son and herself. Every day God gave her oil and flour because she'd shared what little she had.

Bathtime for Pepper

One day  and  went to  's house. They were going to help take care of  .

helped  and  give  a  .

After his  ,  used a  to make  's fur shiny. Then it was  's turn.  liked having both  and  use a  on his fur.

 said it was time to take  for a walk.  held 's while they walked around the farm.  held 's when they walked back to 's house.

"I like taking care of dogs," said .

"Me, too,"  said. "Tomorrow, let's take care of my dog."

A Widow Shares What She Has

Bible story based on 1 Kings 17:8–16

In the Bible story, who did Elijah ask for food? Did she have enough? How did God help?

When Mia and Madison were playing together, how did they share? What were some of the ways they took care of Pepper? Who were they going to take care of the following day?

In your family, what are some things you need to share with each other? For example, the TV, the bathroom, food, the couch, etc. Why is it hard to share sometimes? Have you thought about sharing as a way to show kindness to each other? Name some of the ways you have shared with each other today. Now think about ways you can share with others as a family. Are there items in your home that you could give away to others who need them? Or how about inviting a friend over for supper? What other ways can you think of to share with others?

What We Learned About God: God wants us to share what we have.

Let's Pray: Dear God, thank You for everything You have given to us. We are so grateful for all of Your blessings. Please help us to do a better job of sharing what we have with each other. Sharing is a great way to be kind to each other. It's not always about who goes first or who gets the favorite chair. When we share, we honor You. Amen.

Share with the Lord's people who are in need.
Romans 12:13

Daniel and the Lions

Bible story based on Daniel 6

A man named Daniel had a problem. He lived in a country where the people didn't believe in God. In fact, it was against the law to pray to God!

But Daniel prayed to God anyway. He and the king were friends. But the king's other advisors were jealous. So they got Daniel in trouble for praying to God. He was thrown into the lions' den to be eaten.

But God sent angels to shut the mouths of the lions.

The king rushed to the den and saw that God had kept Daniel safe, and he decided to believe in God too. He changed the law in his country and told everyone to believe in the one true God!

Out to Eat!

 and decided to take  and  out for dessert one night. They drove in the  to their favorite place that served 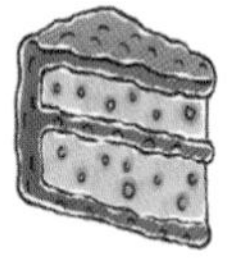 and .

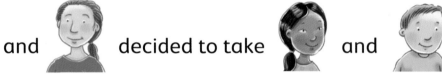

Before they took a bite,  bowed his head to  to God, thanking Him for this special family time. But some other people frowned when they saw him praying.

"I love these , ," said .

"My 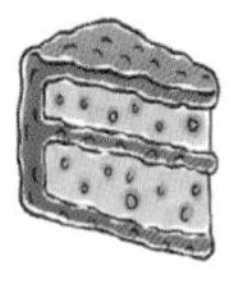 is yummy!" said , who had frosting all over his face.

In the  on the way home,  asked, "Why did those people frown when you bowed your head to , ?"

 said, "Well, not everyone believes in God. But God wants us to help other people know about Him, and that's what we did tonight.

It was bedtime, so  and  brushed their teeth and put on their pajamas. When they were in their beds, it was time to .

 smiled and said, "I'm so glad we can  to our God."

Daniel and the Lions

Bible story based on Daniel 6

In the Bible story, what problem did Daniel have? What did he decide to do anyway? But then what happened to him? Who kept him safe from the lions? When the king saw that Daniel was still alive, what did he do?

When the Scott family decided to go out for dessert, other people at the restaurant frowned at them. Why? When the Scott family was back in the car, what did Mr. Scott say about helping other people know about God?

As a family, talk about when your favorite times to pray are. Has there ever been a time when you have prayed in a public place and people noticed what you were doing? Talk about those experiences together. Remember that no matter what, we should always be able to show our faith in God. It's a great way to let other people know about Him.

What We Learned about God: We can help others know about God.

Let's Pray: Dear God, saying this prayer to You right now feels extra special because of what we just learned in these stories. Help us be like Daniel and have the courage to show our faith in You, even in front of other people who don't know You yet. May these people become curious about You, and may our actions lead them to want to know more about You. Amen.

Call to me and I will answer you and tell you great and unsearchable things you do not know.
Jeremiah 33:3

Jonah Learns to Obey

Bible story based on Jonah 1–3

1. God told Jonah to go and talk to the people of Nineveh. But Jonah didn't. He got into a boat going away from Nineveh.

2. God made a big storm on the sea. Soon Jonah was in the water, but God sent a big fish to save Jonah. The fish opened its mouth and swallowed him.

3. Jonah prayed, and God made the fish spit Jonah out onto dry land. Now Jonah was ready to obey God. He went to Nineveh.

4. Jonah told everyone in Nineveh to love God by obeying Him. The people asked God to forgive them for not obeying. And God forgave them.

Time for a Snack

 was hungry.  left  for a snack.

 But  didn't want . He wanted .

So  stood on a tall stool to reach the .

As he grabbed the , he knocked over a cup of 

and splashed  all over the floor.

 "Oops," said .

Just then  came in and saw the mess.

", what are you doing?"  asked.

 said, "I climbed up to get , and I spilled the ."

"You know  left  for a snack," said . "Put the back, and I'll help you clean up."

As they cleaned up the mess,  thanked . "Thanks for helping me clean up my mess. I should have obeyed ."

 answered, " wants us to obey him. When we 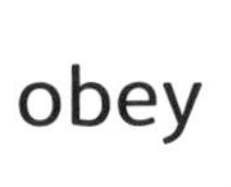obey , we show our love for him."

Jonah Learns to Obey

Bible story based on Jonah 1–3

Jonah said no to God. What had God asked him to do? What happened to Jonah? When the people in Nineveh heard what Jonah had to say, what did they do? Did God forgive them?

What did Mr. Mitchell leave for his boys to eat as a snack? What did Isaac want to eat instead? What happened when Isaac didn't obey? How did Caleb help? What reminder did he give Isaac?

In your family, think about times when your mom or dad has asked you to obey a rule that was hard to follow. Feel free to share examples of this with each other. Why was it so hard to obey that rule? But why is it important to obey? Building trust with each other is important. Then we know we can count on each other no matter what.

What We Learned about God: Obedience shows we love God.

Let's Pray: Dear God, we know that we can trust You completely. Please help us build trust with each other. When we need to obey, please help us be strong and do the right thing. We love You, Lord. Help us to be more like You. Amen.

If you love me, keep my commands.
John 14:15

An Angel Tells of Jesus's Birth

Bible story based on Matthew 1:18–25; Luke 1:26–38

1. One day something wonderful happened to Mary. An angel told her, "God has a special plan for you. You will have a baby. He will be God's Son."

2. Mary believed in God's plan for her. She said she would do all that God wanted her to do for Jesus's coming.

3. One night an angel came to see Joseph, too. The angel said, "Take Mary as your wife. She will have a special baby. Name Him Jesus."

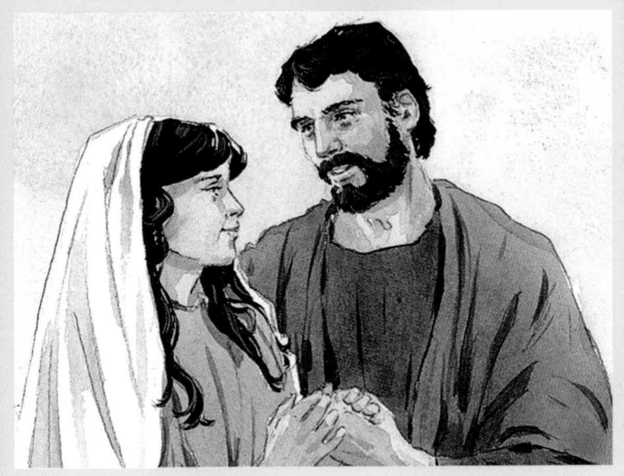

4. Joseph believed the angel. So he took Mary as his wife. Joseph would name Mary's child Jesus. What special news: Jesus was coming!

The Big Surprise

On Monday, Kaden ran down the steps. Mr. and Mrs. Young were talking in the kitchen. When he came into the room, they stopped. Kaden wondered why.

On Tuesday, Madison heard something in the bedroom. When she went in, her mom was closing the closet door. She wondered what her mom was hiding.

On Wednesday night, Mr. Young drove the car away. Kaden asked, "Why didn't Dad take me along?"

"He might be out past your bedtime," said his mom. Kaden was sure his mom and dad must be getting a surprise ready. What were they up to?

On Thursday, Mrs. Young ran down to the basement. Kaden and Madison whispered, "Whatever Mom and Dad are getting ready must be all over the house."

On Friday night, Mr. Young came home with pizza, just like he always did. But he said, "I need help with something in the car. It's a surprise."

Kaden said, "Now we'll find out what you've been getting ready!"

The car was filled with wood. Mr. Young said, "This year we're going to make a manger for the yard and a sign to tell people to get ready, because Jesus is coming."

"Wow! How will we make it?" asked Madison.

"With these." Mrs. Young gave Madison and Kaden each a bag. "I hid these bags in my closet all week." Each bag held a hammer and a paint brush. "The paint is in the basement," she added.

"Can we start tonight?" asked Kaden.

"Yes," said his dad. "But first, let's eat our pizza!"

Family Talk Time

An Angel Tells of Jesus's Birth

Bible story based on Matthew 1:18–25; Luke 1:26–38

In the Bible story, who came to see Mary? What did the angel tell Mary? Who else did the angel tell? What would the baby's name be? Yes! Jesus would soon be born!

Mr. and Mrs. Young were planning something big for Christmastime. But it was a secret! When Mr. Young came home with the pizza, what was in the car? What were they going to make in order to tell others about Jesus?

Christmastime is such a special time of the year. It's a time when we look forward to spending time together as a family, eating special food, and giving each other presents. With all the fun going on at this time of year, our days get very busy. Let's remind each other that the whole reason we are celebrating is because of the most special gift we will ever receive. Do you know what, or Who, that is? Yes, it's Jesus!

What We Learned about God: Jesus is coming.

Let's Pray: Dear God, thank You for sending Your Son, Jesus, into the world. As Christmas gets closer and closer, help us to never forget why we celebrate this special time of the year. Help us look forward to Christmas Day, when we remember the most special gift we will ever receive—Jesus! Amen.

God sent his Son.
Galatians 4:4

Jesus Is Born in Bethlehem

Bible story based on Luke 2:1–7

Clip, clop. Clip, clop. A donkey walked slowly along the road. Mary and Joseph were going to Bethlehem to be counted. The king wanted to know how many people lived in the land.

It was a long trip for Mary. Soon she was going to have a special baby. This was the baby the angel had told her about.

When they came to Bethlehem, Joseph tried to find a room for them. All the rooms were full. But there was one place where they could stay. It was in a stable with some animals.

That night Mary had a baby boy! Mary and Joseph named the baby Jesus, just as the angel had told them to do. They were happy. They knew that this little baby was God's Son.

Piñata Party

 and her family were in a rush! "Hurry!" said .

"Why?" asked .  was too busy to answer.

"Hurry!" said . "Get the ."

"Why?" asked .  was too busy to answer.

"Hurry!" said . "Put on your new ."

Now  knew why everyone was in a hurry. It was almost time for the  party! 's family had birthday parties with a  . And today was a special birthday.

Soon the house was full of people, and it was time to break  open the  with a stick. Inside the  was  .

 said, "Before we break open the  , I have a question. Why are we having this party?"

Everyone shouted, "We're having a party for Jesus's birthday!"

Then  took the stick, put on the blindfold, and broke open the  on her first try! The  flew out of the  , and everyone picked up some pieces.

Jesus Is Born in Bethlehem

Bible story based on Luke 2:1-7

When it was almost time for Mary to have baby Jesus, where did she travel to with Joseph? Did they find a room to stay overnight? Where did they stay instead? Then what happened? Yes! Baby Jesus was born!

How did the Lopez family celebrate Jesus's birthday? What was inside the piñata? What are some ways Sophia knew this was a special party?

As a family, share some ideas with each other about what you can do this year to celebrate the birth of Jesus in a special way. Vote on the top ideas and then put your party plans together!

What We Learned about God: Jesus was born!

Let's Pray: Dear Jesus, thank You for coming to the world as a tiny baby. May we always remember that special Christmas night when You were born in a stable in Bethlehem. Help us keep You as the most special and important part of Christmas every year. Amen.

She gave birth to her firstborn, a son. She wrapped him in cloths and placed him in a manger.
Luke 2:7

Shepherds Tell about Jesus

Bible story based on Luke 2:8–20

1. Bible-time shepherds often stayed outside day and night. They kept their sheep safe. They made sure the sheep had food and water.

2. One night an angel said, "I have good news. God's Son, Jesus, has been born. He's in a manger." Then many angels came and began praising God.

3. The angels left, and the shepherds ran to find Jesus. He was lying in a manger, just as the angel had said. The shepherds worshipped Him.

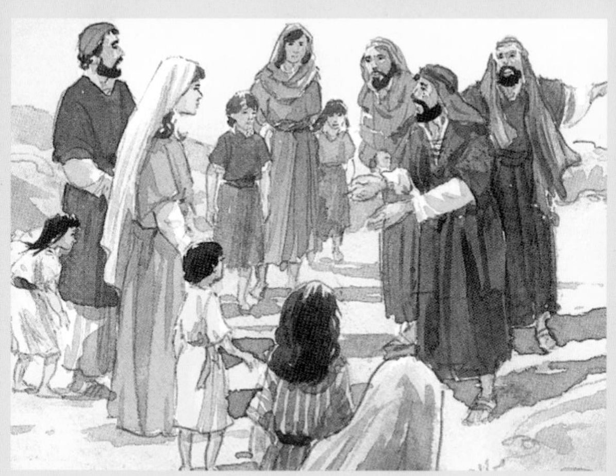

4. On the way back to their sheep, the shepherds told everyone they met about Jesus.

A Christmas Pageant

It's time to tell our story.
Look at all the children!
They're telling the story of baby Jesus!

Shepherds Tell about Jesus

Bible story based on Luke 2:8–20

In the Bible story, shepherds were watching their sheep one night. Who came to tell them good news? What was the good news? So what did the shepherds do?

What were the children getting ready to do? Name a few of the parts they played in the Christmas pageant. This is a great way to tell others about Jesus. Many churches have Christmas programs like this. What a great time to invite neighbors and friends!

Do you remember ever watching a Christmas pageant with your family? Or have any of you been in one before? If so, talk about what part you played and what it was like. Consider doing one as a family. Someone can volunteer to read Luke 2 as you act it out. What are some ways you can tell others about Jesus?

What We Learned about God: We can tell others about Jesus.

Let's Pray: Dear God, Christmas is such a wonderful time of the year when we can celebrate the birth of Jesus. Help us find ways to tell others about Jesus because we want everyone to know about the best and greatest gift of all time! Amen.

A Savior has been born to you; he is the Messiah, the Lord.
Luke 2:11

Simeon and Anna Meet Jesus

Bible story based on Luke 2:21–38

When Jesus was a tiny baby, Mary and Joseph took Him to the temple. They wanted to thank God for sending Jesus. They also had a special offering to bring to the temple.

Later an old man, Simeon, saw Jesus at the temple. God helped Simeon know that Jesus was God's Son. Simeon held baby Jesus and prayed, "Thank You, God, for letting me see Your Son."

Just then an older woman named Anna came over to see the baby. God also helped Anna know that Jesus was God's Son.

Simeon and Anna were happy. Everywhere they went, they told people that Jesus was God's Son.

Just Like Dad

Isaac, Caleb, and their father, Mr. Mitchell, went to visit Nana.

Isaac was the first one to Nana's door. Nana opened the door. She said, "Steve! I'm glad to see you."

"Steve?" said Isaac. "I'm Isaac."

Nana said, "You look so much like your dad I called you by his first name."

Isaac looked at his dad. His dad was six feet tall and had brown hair. He didn't look like Isaac at all!

Nana found a photo album. She said, "Look at these pictures."

Isaac looked and saw a picture of a boy. He asked, "Where did you get this picture of me?"

Mr. Mitchell laughed. "That's me! When I was five years old, I looked a lot like you do. That's why Nana called you Steve."

Nana said, "Steve was a good son. He still is! You boys are just like him."

Isaac was glad Nana said he and Caleb were like Dad. He thought his father was pretty special.

Caleb pointed to the manger scene on Nana's table. "Isaac, do you know whose Son Jesus is?

"Yes," said Isaac. "Jesus is God's Son!"

Mr. Mitchell said, "And God's Son, Jesus, came to let us know what God is like!"

Family Talk Time

Simeon and Anna Meet Jesus

Bible story based on Luke 2:21–38

In the Bible story, where did Mary and Joseph bring Jesus when He was a tiny baby? Who were the elderly people who had been waiting to see Him? What did they know to be true about Jesus?

Isaac and Caleb went to visit someone with their dad. Who was it? When Nana saw Isaac, what name did she call him by mistake? Why? What book did they look at together? Then what did they see on Nana's table?

As a family, share ways you are alike in how you talk, what you look like, expressions on your face, habits you have, favorite foods. What else? Now think about Jesus. When we are behaving like Jesus did, what are some things we do?

What We Learned about God: Jesus is God's Son.

Let's Pray: Dear God, thank You for sending Jesus to the world so that we can better know what You are like. Thank You for our family. Each one of us belongs right here in this house, right where You planned we would be. Thank You also for the gift of being part of *Your* family, God. Thank You for sending Your Son, Jesus, as our Savior. Because of Jesus, we know how to be like Him and follow Your ways. Amen.

My eyes have seen your salvation.
Luke 2:30

Wise Men Worship Jesus

Bible story based on Matthew 2:1–11

1. "A new star!" shouted a wise man one night, looking up in the sky. "It means a king has been born! A king from God on high!"

2. "We must go to find this king!" The wise men all agreed, so they started on their trip, knowing the star would lead the way.

3. The wise men found the King! Their hearts were filled with joy. They brought their gifts to Jesus and worshipped the little boy.

4. "We knew that we would find Him. We followed after His star. And now we've worshipped the King. How full of joy we are!"

The Late Present

Michael didn't want to go to Sunday school. "I forgot to give my present to Mr. and Mrs. Young before we went away for Christmas," he said. "Now it's too late to give them the book about Jesus."

"It's not too late," said his mom. "Bring the present. You'll see."

Michael didn't say anything at Sunday school. He hid the present under his shirt so no one could see it.

Michael didn't play with his friends either. He couldn't make stars with his friends, because every time he moved, the present poked him in the stomach.

He didn't help look for something Mrs. Young asked the class to find, because the present might fall on the floor if he bent over. Michael just watched.

Finally it was time for the Bible story. Michael carefully sat down so the present wouldn't poke him in the arms.

Mrs. Young told a story about camels and wise men in Bible times. The wise men brought presents to Jesus.

Kaden asked, "Did they bring presents for Jesus's birthday?"

Mrs. Young said, "They brought the presents to worship Jesus, because He is God's Son. Since they traveled on camels, it took them a long time to get to Jesus's house. It was a long time after His birthday when they got there."

"You mean the present was late?" asked Michael.

Mr. Young smiled. "Jesus didn't mind. He knew the wise men came as fast as they could. It wasn't too late to worship Jesus."

Michael stood up and pulled out his present. He said, "This is for you, Mr. and Mrs. Young."

"Thank you, Michael!" said Mrs. Young. She unwrapped the present and read a story about Jesus from the new book he had given them.

Michael was glad he had brought the present to Sunday school. Everyone in the class was able to worship Jesus by listening to the Bible story.

Wise Men Worship Jesus

Bible story based on Matthew 2:1–11

What did the wise men see up in the sky? What did this mean? So where did they go? Do you know what presents the wise men gave Jesus? (Gold, frankincense, and myrrh.) This was their way of worshipping Jesus.

Why didn't Michael want to go to Sunday school? What was he hiding under his shirt? Were Mr. and Mrs. Young mad that his gift was late? Why not? How was the timing of Michael's gift like the timing of the gifts the wise men gave Jesus?

As a family, think about the ways you worship Jesus. What are some things you do? (Pray, go to Sunday school, go to church, sing praise songs, have devotional time, etc.) Share your favorite ways to worship. Have a special family worship time, with each person choosing a favorite way to be part of this worship.

What We Learned about God: We can worship Jesus.

Let's Pray: Dear God, we're so thankful You sent Jesus to save us from our sins. We worship You and praise Your holy name. We want to use the gifts You have given to us as a way to express our joy to You. When we worship You, help us to not worry about what other people might think, but free us up to show You how much we love You in our own special ways. Amen.

Where is the one who has been born king of the Jews? We saw his star when it rose and have come to worship him.
Matthew 2:2

Jesus Goes to the Temple

Bible story based on Luke 2:40–52

1. Jesus grew and learned to help Joseph. When He was twelve years old, he joined his parents on a special trip to the temple in Jerusalem.

2. It was a long way to Jerusalem. Jesus walked with His family and friends. When they got there, everyone worshipped God.

3. When they left to go back home, Mary and Joseph thought Jesus was with His friends. He wasn't! They went back to the temple to find Him.

4. Jesus was there, talking with the teachers. He said, "I had to talk with the teachers about God." Then Jesus went home with Joseph and Mary.

Learning More

By listening at church. I learn a lot when we do activities and read Bible stories. It's fun too!

What did you learn today, Ava? Maybe Dad will read us the Bible story when we finish lunch.
I like Bible stories too.

Those sound like great ideas, Evan. I'm glad you want to grow and learn more about God, just like Jesus grew and learned. And I'm glad you want to help Ava learn too.

Family Talk Time

Jesus Goes to the Temple

Bible story based on Luke 2:40–52

Do you remember how old Jesus was when He went to the temple in Jerusalem? How much older or younger is that than you are? What did Jesus do at the temple with His family and friends? What happened when it was time to leave? Where was Jesus?

When the Li family talked about Jesus going to the temple as a boy, why did Mr. Li think Jesus stayed there longer? How does the Li family learn about God?

Now think about the ways your own family learns about God. Are your ways similar to the Li family's? What is different? What are some of your favorite ways to learn about God and why? Do you have other ideas for how your family can learn about God? Try a few new ways this week.

What We Learned about God: Jesus grew and learned.

Let's Pray: Dear God, help us learn as much as we can about You. We want to know as much as we can so that our hearts will show Your love and so that we can understand what it means to be a Christian. Please help our family keep learning about You however we can, Lord. Amen.

And Jesus grew in wisdom and stature,
and in favor with God and man.
Luke 2:52

Jesus Is Baptized

Bible story based on Matthew 3:13–17; John 1:32–34

Jesus grew up and became a man. He was ready to do His important work.

Jesus went to the Jordan River to be baptized. He asked John the Baptist to baptize Him at the river.

John didn't think he was good enough to baptize Jesus. But Jesus said it was the right thing for him to do. So John did.

When Jesus came out of the water, God spoke from heaven! He said, "This is My Son, and I love Him. I am very pleased with Him."

Silly Boots

"Silly ," said. He threw his as walked by.

"Hey!" said. "Why did you throw your ?"

said, "I can't get my to fit. And I have to wear

them to play in the !"

asked, "Are those your new ?"

"Yes. Let me show you the problem," said, putting the

on again.

"Wait," said  . "Look at your  . They aren't on the right feet."

 said he was sorry. "Did  ever put his  on wrong?"

"Yes," answered  . "Your dad learned, and you will too. God helps us learn new things. We make God  when we use what we learn to help others."

 was glad God helped him learn new things.  and  helped  shovel  . "Am I making God  now,  ?"  asked.

"Yes, you are!"  replied.

Family Talk Time

Jesus Is Baptized

Bible story based on Matthew 3:13–17; John 1:32–34

When Jesus grew up to be a man, He went to the Jordan River. What happened there? Who was John? God actually spoke on that day. Do you remember what God said about Jesus?

What was the problem with Kaden's boots? Why was he putting them on? Who did he help with shoveling? How did this please God?

God is pleased when we live like Jesus did and when we make good decisions like Jesus did. When you think about this week as a family, what are some ways you can please God? Remember that it's not just what you do but how you do it. For example, is it better to be a grumpy helper or a happy helper? (You may also want to talk about baptism and what your family tradition is for baptism.)

You can do the activity at the back of the book as a reminder for how each of you belong in your family.

What We Learned about God: Jesus pleased God.

Let's Pray: Dear God, thank You for showing us how we should live by sending Jesus as our example. Help us try to live like Jesus, because we want to please You, Lord. We know that this means not just doing good things but also doing them with the right attitude. Amen.

This is my Son, whom I love; with him I am well pleased.
Matthew 3:17

Jesus Calls Four Fishermen

Bible story based on Matthew 4:18–22; Luke 5:1–11

1. Jesus wanted to teach people about God. He got into Peter's boat and asked him to row out a ways. Then everyone could see Him.

2. Later Jesus said to Peter, "Row out to deeper water. Let down your net." Peter didn't think he would catch any fish, but he obeyed Jesus.

3. Peter and his brother Andrew caught so many fish that they needed help. James and John helped them bring the fish into the boat.

4. Jesus told the fishermen, "Follow Me, and find people instead of fish." So Peter, Andrew, James, and John left everything to do what Jesus said.

Follow the Leader

At [church], the children played Follow the Leader during Sunday school.

One Sunday, [Mia] was the leader. [Mia] led the class to the story circle.

On another Sunday, [Pastor Bennet] came to class. [Mrs. Young] said, "Will you be our leader today?"

 said, "Yes." He opened his  and sat down. The kids sat down too.  . Everyone said the words after him.

 said, "You followed . You , just like  wants you to do."

 said, "You came to , just like  wants you to do. You learn from the . You learn to obey  all week long. You follow  by obeying Him.  is the best leader of all!"

Jesus Calls Four Fishermen

Bible story based on Matthew 4:18–22; Luke 5:1–11

In the Bible story, what was Jesus standing in when He was teaching the people? Jesus told Peter and Andrew to fish with their nets. Did they catch anything? What did Jesus ask them to do instead of catch fish?

What game did the children play at church? Who were the leaders in the Sunday school class? What did Pastor Bennet teach the children? How did they follow Jesus?

As a family, how do you follow Jesus? What are some things you do at home to show this? Do your neighbors know that you follow Jesus? How? What about at school or other public places? Would people know that you follow Jesus? Why is it important that people know this?

What We Learned about God: Jesus said, "Follow Me."

Let's Pray: Dear Jesus, we want to follow You. May our lives show that we follow You in how we treat each other and how we treat others. Help us make this our most important goal as a family, to follow You as our leader in everything we do. Amen.

"Come, follow me," Jesus said,
"and I will send you out to fish for people."
Matthew 4:19

Down through the Roof

Bible story based on Mark 2:1–12

1. There was a man who could not walk. He was very sad because he had to lie down all day on a mat.

2. The man had four good friends who helped him. They took him to see Jesus. But too many other people wanted to see Jesus too.

3. The four friends made a hole in the roof of the house where Jesus was. They lowered the man into the house.

4. Jesus made the man well. The man could walk. The man was very glad his four good friends brought him to Jesus!

Sophia Needs a Ride

 took  to .  was happy. Her  were going to sing in  .

 looked around. Someone was missing.  was missing!

 saw  at school.  said, "We missed you at practice, ."

 looked sad. She said, “I can’t come anymore. I can’t get to .”

 said, “We need you to help us sing in .”  knew who could help.  said, “I’ll ask  if we can help.”

 said, “We can take  to . We can help our .”

Down through the Roof

Bible story based on Mark 2:1–12

In the Bible story, a man couldn't walk. Who took him to see Jesus? When they got to the house, what was the problem? So what did the friends do? What did Jesus do for the man?

Why was Mia happy? But then what did she find out about Sophia? How did Mia and her mom help?

Friends are important. We see that in the two stories we just read together. There was no way the man who couldn't walk could have gotten to Jesus. And look what happened. His friends carried him to Jesus, and that changed his life forever! And Sophia couldn't get to church, but Mia and her mom offered to give her rides. Share together how you've helped a friend recently or how a friend has helped you. How does it make you feel when you help a friend or a friend helps you?

What We Learned about God: Friends help each other.

Let's Pray: Dear God, thank You for friends. Sometimes we can help them, and sometimes they can help us—all because we care about each other. When You lived on the earth, You showed us what it means to be a friend. May we try our best to be good friends to others. Amen.

Carry each other's burdens, and in this way
you will fulfill the law of Christ.
Galatians 6:2

Jesus Teaches about God's Love

Bible story based on Matthew 6:25–34; Luke 12:22–31

Many people came to hear Jesus teach about God. Jesus said, "Don't worry about food. See the birds? God feeds the birds. He will feed you, too. God loves you more than the birds. Trust God's love."

Then Jesus said, "Don't worry about clothes. See the flowers? The flowers wear beautiful colors. God gives flowers their colors. And He'll help you have clothes. He loves you more than flowers."

Just in Case

Aunt Carla, I'm so glad you're finally here. Now we can go for our hike. What do you have?
I'm glad I could come with you, Sophia. I brought sandwiches.

Why?
In case we get hungry.

Mama, why are we taking lemonade?
In case we get thirsty. Will you please get our big, furry blanket?

Why?
In case we get tired.

Bugs
Are you really going to take your insect book, Alex? You take it everywhere.
Yes, I am. I might see a bug I want to find in my book.

I'm hungry!
I'm thirsty!
What a great spot to stop and have a picnic. I needed to rest.
We needed everything we brought.

Hey, that's a ladybug. My *book* says ladybugs eat insects that are harmful.
I guess God gives us everything we need to live ... including ladybugs.

Family Talk Time

Jesus Teaches about God's Love

Bible story based on Matthew 6:25–34; Luke 12:22–31

In the Bible story, when Jesus was teaching the people in Bible times, He said God loves them more than what? Did he tell them it's okay to be worried? Why not?

What were Sophia and her family getting ready to do? Name some of the items they brought with them on their hike. What insect did Alex find?

Sit down together as a family. Take time to share with each other some of the things you worry about. Remember what Jesus said—that we don't have to worry. Then share how you give your worries to God. What are some ways you do that? You can help encourage each other.

What We Learned about God: God knows what we need.

Let's Pray: Dear Lord, help us remember what You taught us in the Bible about worrying. May we give our worries to You because You know what we need. You are in control of everything. Help us trust in You completely for everything. When we see the birds and flowers, let them be a reminder that if You care for them, You also care for us. Amen.

Do not worry about your life, what you will eat or drink; or about your body, what you will wear.
Matthew 6:25

Jesus Helps an Important Man

Bible story based on Luke 7:1–10

One day a centurion sent someone to get help from Jesus. The centurion's servant was very sick.

Jesus said He would go to the man. The people who were following Him went along too.

When Jesus was almost there, the centurion sent more people to Jesus. They said, "You don't need to come all the way to the house. The centurion knows You can help his sick servant from where You are now."

Jesus said, "I never met anyone who believed in Me so much!" So Jesus didn't go to the house.

The centurion was right. Jesus made the servant well without even seeing him! Jesus helped the centurion's servant.

The Littlest Puppy

loved her dog  . One day,  had  .

told  , "I think the littlest  is sick."

was sad.

said, "  can help the  ." He prayed, "Dear

, please help the  feel better."

Two days later,  came to  's  .  said,

"How is the  ?"

 said, "I'm happy!  helped the . We took the  to the animal doctor. Now he has . You can play with the  now."

 said, "I'm glad the  is growing big and strong."

Jesus Helps an Important Man

Bible story based on Luke 7:1–10

In the Bible story, who was very sick? How did Jesus find out about it? What happened when He was on his way to the centurion's house? What did Jesus say? And then what did He do for the sick servant before He even got to the house?

What did Mia's dog have? What was wrong with the littlest puppy? What did her friend Michael do? Where did Mia and her family take the puppy? When Michael came over again two days later, how was the puppy? What did Mia tell Michael about playing with the puppy?

As a family, think about your friends again. What's the best way to ask Jesus to help them? Yes, by praying. God wants to hear our prayers. He wants us to talk to Him. He can answer our prayers and help the people we pray for. How often do you pray for your friends?

What We Learned about God: Jesus can help our friends.

Let's Pray: Dear God, we know that You care about us and that You are interested in what is going on in our lives. Help us remember to pray for our friends. Sometimes there is nothing we can do, like when they get sick or if they have to move away. But You are with them, Lord. And You have the power to help them in all ways. Help us remember that. Amen.

Now faith is confidence in what we hope for and assurance about what we do not see.
Hebrews 11:1

Jesus Stops the Storm

Bible story based on Mark 4:35–41

1. One day Jesus was busy teaching people about God. When He finished, He said to His disciples, "Let's go over to the other side of the lake."

2. Jesus was tired, so He fell asleep. Soon the sky grew dark. The wind blew, and big waves crashed into the boat. The disciples were afraid.

3. The scared men woke Jesus up. But Jesus wasn't scared. He stood up and said to the storm, "Quiet! Be still!" Right away the storm stopped.

4. Jesus said to His disciples, "Why were you afraid? Didn't you know I would keep you safe?" They were learning that Jesus can do anything.

Singing in the Truck

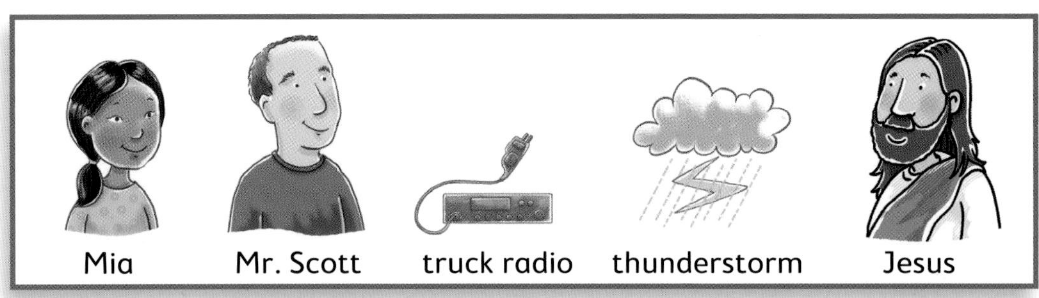

Sometimes  's dad took her for rides in his big truck.  liked listening to her dad talk on his 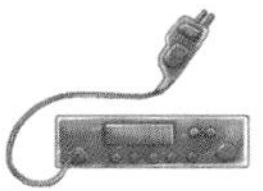 to other truck drivers.

One day  and  were driving in a  .

 said, "I'm scared."

said, "Me, too. Can you sing the song you learned in Sunday school?"

 sang, "When you're scared or worried,  can help you.  can do anything; if you ask Him to." *

 said, "That song is just right for a . Let me sing with you."

Soon a man spoke on the . "Your song is helping me feel better about the . Keep singing."

 smiled. She liked being on the . and  sang until they got home.

"I'm glad you're home," said 's mom. "That was a bad . But I know  can do anything."

"We sang about that all the way home," said . She told her mom about being on the .

** Sung to the tune of "Row, Row, Row Your Boat."*

Jesus Stops the Storm

Bible story based on Mark 4:35–41

In the Bible story, Jesus and His disciples were in a boat so they could get to the other side of the lake. But what happened? Jesus had been sleeping, but the disciples woke Him up. What did Jesus say to the storm? Jesus asked the disciples why they were afraid. After all, Jesus can do anything!

Mia's dad was a truck driver. What did she like to listen to him do? One day they were riding together in the truck, and Mia got scared. Why? What did she do? What was the song about? When Jesus can do anything, we don't need to be afraid.

As a family, think about some things that scare you. Share a few examples with each other. We learned from the Bible story and Mia's story that it doesn't help to be scared. Why not? As a reminder to your family, work together to create a mini poster or sign that you can put on the refrigerator that says "Jesus can do anything." And consider making one for your car, too, so that others can see and remember this too.

What We Learned about God: Jesus can do anything.

Let's Pray: Dear God, sometimes we get scared. Yet we know that You can do anything. Please help us replace being scared with having stronger faith in You. Whatever we're afraid of, help us remember that You are here with us. You will help us. And we don't need to be scared. Amen.

Who is this? Even the wind and the waves obey him!
Mark 4:41

Jesus Feeds Five Thousand People

Bible story based on John 6:5–13

1. A big crowd of people spent the whole day listening to Jesus. Jesus asked Philip, one of His disciples, "Where can we get food for all these people?"

2. A little boy told another disciple named Andrew that he would share his lunch. There were two fish and five loaves of bread—not nearly enough for everyone.

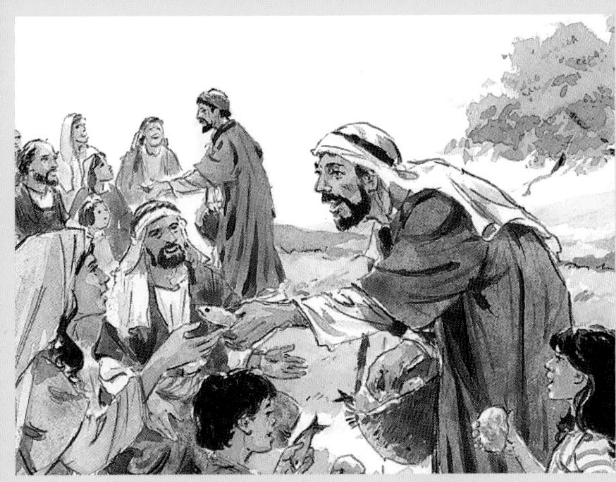

3. Jesus thanked God for the food. Then a miracle happened. His disciples gave fish and bread to *all* of the people.

4. The people ate as much as they wanted. There were even leftovers! The little boy was glad Jesus used his lunch to feed the people.

Food from Empty Cans

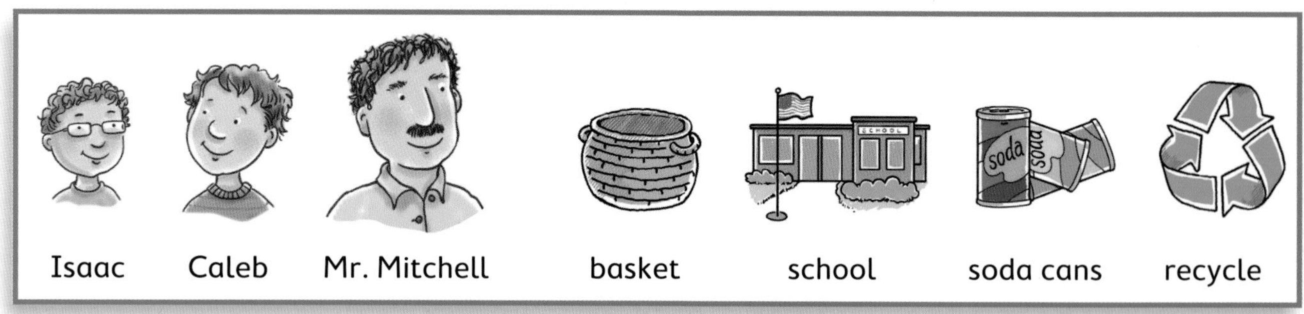

"What is the  at church for?"  asked.

 said, "We'll fill the  with food for people who don't have any."

 asked, "What can I put in the  ?"

"You can put cans of food in the  ,"  said.

 wondered how he could get money to buy food.

 and  cleaned the playground after .

 said, “Keep the 

. We can  them for money.”

When the playground was clean,  looked for 

at the park.  and  collected five bags of 

! They were able to  the 

for money.  took  to the store.  bought cans of food. On Sunday,  and  put food in the .  thanked God that he could share.

Family Talk Time

Jesus Feeds Five Thousand People

Bible story based on John 6:5–13

A large crowd came to listen to Jesus in the Bible story. But they got hungry. Who offered to share his lunch? Was it enough for all the people? Why? After Jesus said a prayer of thanks, everyone ate the food, all because a little boy was willing to share.

What was the Mitchell family going to do with the basket? How were they going to get money to buy food? Where did they go to collect cans? And then what did they do? Did it work?

Together, think about things you have that you can share. Are there toys you can share with a neighbor? Or how about inviting someone over for supper? Plan to share something you have with someone else this week. And don't forget to pray for Jesus to bless how you are sharing and to use it in big ways.

What We Learned about God: Jesus can help us share.

Let's Pray: Dear God, when we get busy, sometimes we forget to think of others. Please help us look for ways to help others this week by sharing. Help us take the time to think about those around us and how we can share what we have with them. It doesn't have to be a thing that we share. We could also share our time with someone. Please lead us to find ways to share with someone else this week. Amen.

I am the bread of life. Whoever comes to me will never go hungry, and whoever believes in me will never be thirsty.
John 6:35

Jesus Wants Peter to Trust Him

Bible story based on Matthew 14:22–33

1. Jesus told the disciples to row to the other side of the Sea of Galilee. The waves and the wind made it difficult to row.

2. Jesus walked on the water to the disciples. They were scared, because at first they didn't know it was Jesus.

3. Peter trusted Jesus to help him walk on the water too. Jesus said, "Come," because He wanted Peter to trust Him. Because he trusted Jesus, Peter was able to walk on the water.

4. But Peter stopped trusting Jesus, so he started to sink. Jesus helped Peter back into the boat. The disciples worshipped Jesus because they believed they could trust Him.

The Swimming Lesson

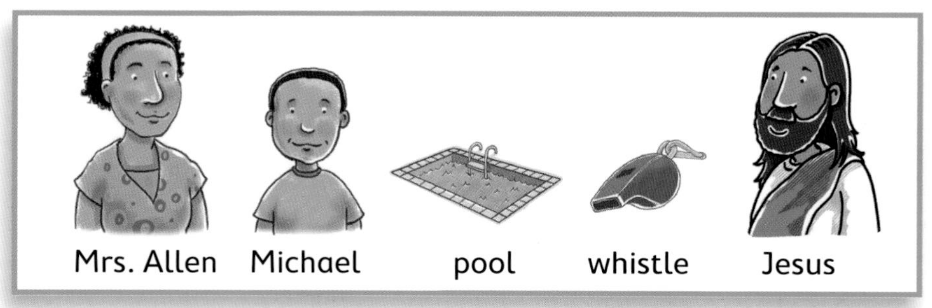

 signed  up for swimming lessons.  thought it would be fun to swim across a .

 took  to his first lesson.  looked at the . It was big! How could he ever swim across it? He heard a [whistle]. It was time to swim!

 was afraid of how big the  was. He thought of when  walked on the water. " walked on water. I

can trust  to help me swim."  prayed, "Dear , I trust You to help me. I know You can do anything."

 joined the kids in the  when the teacher blew the  again. The teacher showed them many things.

After the lesson,  knew one day he would swim across the .

Jesus Wants Peter to Trust Him

Bible story based on Matthew 14:22–33

In the Bible story, the disciples were rowing a boat on the Sea of Galilee. What made it difficult to row? Who walked on the water to the disciples? And who joined Him? Why did Peter start to sink?

When we were hearing about the Allen family, who started going to swimming lessons? Why was Michael afraid of the pool? What prayer did he say to Jesus? Did that help?

One of the most important things you can learn as a family and on your own is to trust Jesus. Why do you think that is so important? In the Bible story, Peter was brave to step out of the boat. And Michael learned to trust Jesus as he was learning how to swim. What are some difficult things you are facing right now? Share them with each other. Have you been trusting Jesus as you go through them?

What We Learned about God: Jesus wants us to trust Him.

Let's Pray: Dear Jesus, we know that You are in control of everything. But sometimes we forget. When we're facing hard things as a family or on our own, help us remember to put our trust in You. We can depend on You to guide us through anything. It's not up to us to figure it all out. You can help. Lord, please show us how we can help others trust in You too. Amen.

With God all things are possible.
Matthew 19:26

Jesus Helps a Man Believe in Him

Bible story based on John 9:1–38; 20:31

1. There was a man who was born blind. Jesus helped this man believe in God by healing his eyes. Jesus made some mud to put on the man's eyes.

2. Then Jesus said to the man, "Go to a pool of water and wash the mud off." The blind man listened to Jesus. He washed the mud off at a pool.

3. Suddenly, the man could see! He was so excited. He told everyone that a man named Jesus had healed his eyes.

4. The man didn't know that Jesus was God's Son. Later, Jesus helped the man believe.

Everyone Needs Help

 was sad.

"What's wrong?" asked .

 said, "A big kid called me a baby. He made fun of my ."

 said, "That kid made fun of me, too. He's just being mean."

"Why is he so mean?" asked .

 said, "I don't know why he's mean. He might not know

 is God's Son. You can ask  to help the boy believe in Him. And not making fun of the boy's  or being mean to him will help too."

 told  a Bible story. "There was a man who was born blind. He couldn't see with his . He didn't know about . One day  made the man's  well. Then the man believed  was God's Son."

 said, "This boy uses his 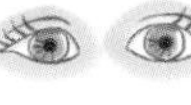 to see, but I know  can help heal the boy's heart so he isn't so mean. I hope the boy will believe in Jesus."

Jesus Helps a Man Believe in Him

Bible story based on John 9:1–38; 20:31

What was wrong with the man in the Bible story? How did Jesus heal his eyes? When the man washed the mud off, what happened? Who did he tell others about?

In the other story, who was getting picked on? What about? What did Caleb think would help the mean boy? What were they going to ask God's to do?

Sometimes we see God working in our lives in amazing ways. Are there some examples that you'd like to share with each other? There are also times when we face hard situations, including mean people, like Isaac did. It's not hard to believe in God when we pay attention and see Him working in our lives, in the good and in the bad. What is the most important thing Jesus did? Yes, He saved us from our sins. How did He do that?

What We Learned about God: Jesus helps us believe in Him.

Let's Pray: Dear Jesus, help us pay attention to what You are doing in our lives. May our faith grow stronger when we see You working through our situations, in the good and in the bad. Keep us strong against temptation, Lord. And thank You for giving us the Bible, where we can learn all about You. Amen.

This is how we know what love is: Jesus Christ laid down his life for us.
1 John 3:16

The Good Shepherd

Bible story based on John 10:1–15

One day Jesus told a story about a shepherd.

Jesus said that in the morning the shepherd called the sheep out of the pen. The sheep knew his voice, and they came whenever he called.

During the day, the shepherd walked ahead of the sheep. He helped them find grass to eat and water to drink. At night he took them safely home again.

The sheep knew that their shepherd loved them. That's why they loved him, too.

Jesus said, "I am like a shepherd. I am the Good Shepherd, and the people who love Me are My sheep. I know each of My sheep by name, and they know Me."

Come, Sheep, Come

The class played a new game at school. One child was the .

All the others were . The  ran all over the yard.

When the  called, "Come, , come," everyone ran to the .

It was 's turn to be the . She stood by the slide. Everyone ran away. When  wasn't looking, a  came up behind her.

 called, "Come, , come." But no one came because they saw the . Then  saw the . She asked Jesus to help her.

 saw the . He ran to . He told the  to go away. When the  ran away,  called, "Come, , come."

All the children ran to him. Then the class went inside.

 said, "I like being a . But Jesus is the best . He sent  to take care of us."

The Good Shepherd

Bible story based on John 10:1–15

In the Bible story, Jesus described a good shepherd. What are some of the things that make a good shepherd? How is Jesus the Good Shepherd? Does He know what your name is?

What game did the children at school play? Who was the shepherd? What animal came up behind her? Who came to help her? Who did Madison say was the best shepherd?

Jesus is a good Shepherd to your family. Think of a few times when you faced a hard situation, and God helped you through it. Now take time to say the following sentence out loud to each person in your family. Make sure that everyone has been included: "______, you are important to Jesus."

What We Learned about God: We are important to Jesus.

Let's Pray: Dear Jesus, thank You for being our Good Shepherd. We know that You love each and every one of us in a special way. Please continue to watch over us and protect us, Lord. We face hard things every day, and we need Your help. Amen.

I am the good shepherd;
I know my sheep and my sheep know me.
John 10:14

Jesus Tells about a Loving Neighbor

Bible story based on Luke 10:25–37

Jesus told this story about neighbors.

As a man walked along a road, some robbers hurt him and took his money. The man needed help.

A priest came by. He taught people about God. But he didn't help the man. The priest wasn't a loving neighbor.

Soon a Levite came by. He helped people worship God. But he didn't help the man. The Levite wasn't a loving neighbor either.

Finally a man from Samaria came by. Most people didn't like Samaritans. They thought Samaritans were bad neighbors. But the Samaritan helped the man. He gave the man some water and took him to a safe place. The Samaritan was a loving neighbor.

Jesus wants us to be loving neighbors too.

Everybody on the Subway!

Sophia and Aunt Carla were visiting the city. They were riding the subway. Sophia saw that there were many people in their subway car.

Sophia quietly said to Aunt Carla, "Look at all the people! Will you please help me count them?"

Aunt Carla smiled. "All right, Sophia. First, count all the children. Then count all the women. Last, count all the men. I'll add the numbers for you."

Sophia looked around the subway car. She looked to the front. She looked behind her. Sophia counted all the babies. She counted all the boys. Then she counted the girls.

Sophia quietly said to Aunt Carla. "There are ten children."

Next Sophia began to count the women. She counted women who were dressed in suits to go to an office. She counted women who were dressed to go to a gym. One woman wore old clothes and a droopy hat and had two shopping bags stuffed with a lot of things.

"Why does that lady have so many bags?" Sophia asked Aunt Carla.

Aunt Carla said, "Some people don't have enough money to buy new clothes. Sometimes they don't have a place to stay, so they carry all their things with them. But Jesus loves the lady with the bags, just as He loves you and me. We must be kind to her just like all the others. All the people are our neighbors."

Sophia finished counting all the women. There were 22 of them.

Then she counted all the men. There were tall men and short men. Some men wore suits. Others wore jeans and T-shirts. There were 16 men in their subway car.

"Aunt Carla said, "That makes 48 people in our subway car!"

Sophia looked around at all the people. She said, "Do you know what, Aunt Carla? They are all my neighbors. I can show love to each one by smiling at them as they walk by me."

Until they got off the subway train in a few stops, Sophia smiled at each person who walked past her.

Jesus Tells about a Loving Neighbor

Bible story based on Luke 10:25–37

In the Bible story, a man was walking along a road. Who came and hurt him and took his money? Other people walked by and saw the hurt man. Do you remember who some of them were? Did they stop to help? Then another man walked by. Did he stop? How did the good Samaritan help the man?

In the story about Sophia, who was she visiting the city with? What were they riding on? What did Sophia decide to do? As she was counting, she realized that all of these people were her neighbors. How did Sophia show love to them as they walked by?

Jesus wants us to be loving neighbors. Pick a couple of ways you can show love to a few of your neighbors throughout the week. Take turns sharing at least two ideas per person. Sometimes simple things like baking a snack or raking a lawn or making a card can make a big difference. Choose the best ideas and make a plan for doing them together as a family.

What We Learned about God: We should show our neighbors we love them.

Let's Pray: Dear God, we see from the Bible story what it means to be a good neighbor. Help us find ways to be good neighbors. Please be with our neighbors, Lord. Whatever their situation, we pray that they will have a close relationship with You. Help us find ways to show our neighbors that we care about them. Amen.

For God so loved the world that he gave his one and only Son.
John 3:16

Jesus Teaches about Prayer

Bible story based on Luke 11:1–4

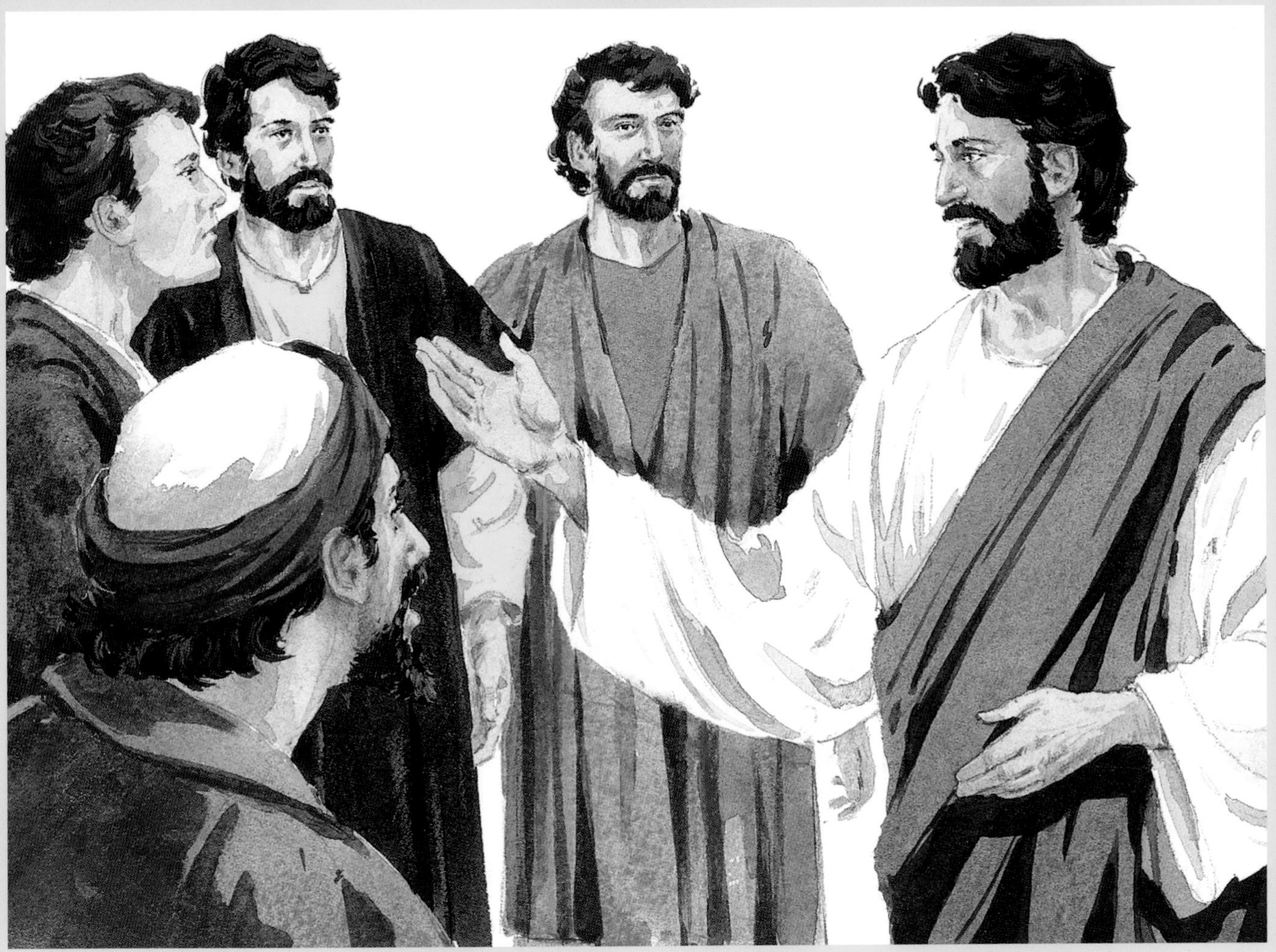

Jesus was praying one day. When He was done, one of His disciples said, "Please teach us how to pray."

So Jesus told His disciples to call God "Father." He said that God is like a father to all who love Him.

Then Jesus said, "You should tell God that you love Him. After that, you can thank God for giving you what you need today.

"You must also ask God to forgive you for things you do wrong.

"And be sure to ask God for help to say no, when you feel like doing something you shouldn't. He can help you do what is right.

"Finish your prayer with 'Amen.'"

Thanking God

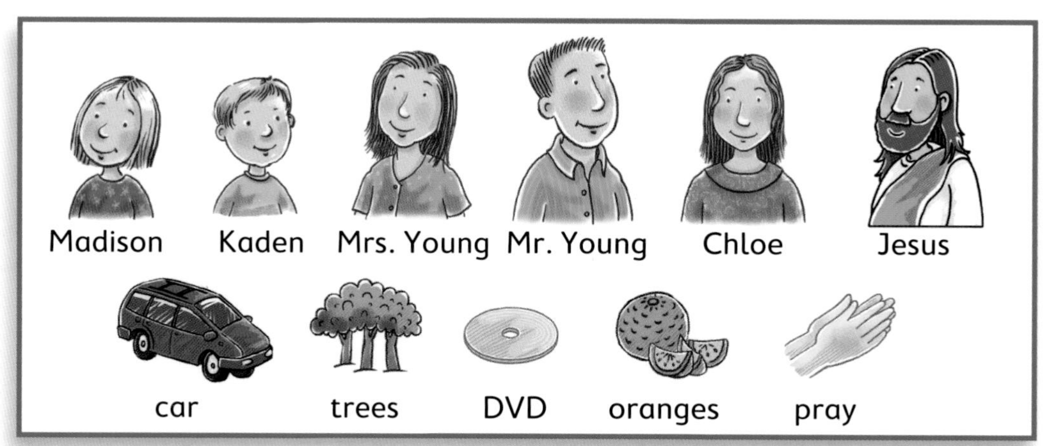

The Young family was going on vacation. In the , they looked for things that showed how great God is.

 saw a lot of . "God must be really great to make so many ."

 and  grew tired of being in the . They fought over what  to watch. But after  helped them

pick out a , they asked God to forgive them for fighting.

 was hungry.  peeled  for a snack. "Hey, I'm thankful for ," said . "Yesterday I learned that  taught us to thank God for giving us what we need."

 said, "That's right.  also taught us the Lord's Prayer. Let's  the Lord's Prayer now. Who can tell me how it starts?"

knew, so they prayed the Lord's Prayer together.

Family Talk Time

Jesus Teaches about Prayer

Bible story based on Luke 11:1–4

In this Bible story, Jesus explains how we should pray. What are some things we should include when we pray? Do you know what this prayer is called in the Bible? Yes, it's the Lord's Prayer.

What was the Young family doing? As they drove in the car, what did they see? And what did they eat as a snack? Were they thankful? What had Madison learned the day before about Whom we should thank for giving us what we need? And how do we do that?

As a family, talk about what prayer is. What are some things you do when you pray? What are some of the things you pray about? One very important thing to pray about is that we are thankful to God. What are you thankful for today? Take turns sharing. Next, try practicing the Lord's Prayer together. This is a great prayer to say together as a family at suppertime.

You can use the Prayer Chart at the back of the book as a reminder for how to pray to God, our loving Father.

What We Learned about God: We can pray to God.

Let's Pray: Our Father in heaven, hallowed be Your name, Your kingdom come, Your will be done, on earth as it is in heaven. Give us today our daily bread. And forgive us our debts, as we also have forgiven our debtors. And lead us not into temptation, but deliver us from the evil one. For thine is the kingdom and the power and the glory. Amen.

Pray continually.
1 Thessalonians 5:17

Little Lost Sheep

Bible story based on Luke 15:1–7

1. A shepherd had one hundred sheep. He loved all of them. He helped them find grass to eat. At night he put them in their pen.

2. Every night the shepherd counted the sheep as they came home. One night the shepherd felt sad. One of the sheep was missing.

3. The shepherd looked and looked. Finally he found the little lost sheep. He was so happy he asked his friends to come over for a party.

4. Jesus said, "I am like that shepherd." Jesus loves each of us just like the shepherd loved each of his sheep.

Lost!

Evan, Ava, please stay close to me. I don't want to lose you.
Sale today
Look at all the colors, Ava!
Red, yellow, green, blue.
What color?
That color is orange, Ava. We need to stay with Mom. We can look for other things that are orange.
Oh no! Mom is gone! We need to stay right here. Mom will find us.
Lost? I want Mommy!

Let's pray and ask God to help Mom find us. Dear Jesus, we know You and Mom love us. Please help Mom find us.

There you are. I'm glad I found you. I love you too much to lose you.
We stayed right here and prayed that God would help you find us.

I'm glad God helped me find you and that you stayed where you were. I wasn't too far away. I just turned the corner and saw that you weren't with me. Let's finish our shopping.

Family Talk Time

Little Lost Sheep

Bible story based on Luke 15:1–7

In the Bible story, do you remember how many sheep the shepherd had? One night when he counted them, one was missing. What did he do? How is Jesus like that?

When Evan and Ava went to the store with their mom, what happened? They were scared, so what did they do? Soon their mom found them. She said she loved them too much to lose them.

As a family, you all love each other very much. When someone gets sick or is sad and needs cheering up, you are there for each other. When we show that kind of love for each other, we are showing the love of Jesus. And we can show that kind of love because Jesus first loved us.

What We Learned about God: Jesus loves us.

Let's Pray: Dear Jesus, thank You for loving us. You know us by name, and You are always there for us. Help us show that same kind of love to each other. We know that someday we'll see You in heaven. Until then, please help us spread Your love to others, so they can learn about You. Amen.

[Jesus] went around doing good.
Acts 10:38

The Father Who Forgave His Son

Bible story based on Luke 15:11–24

1. Jesus told a story about a man who loved his sons. One day the younger son said, "Father, I want the money you have for me now."

2. The son went far away from home. He spent his money on parties and never worked. Soon his money was gone, and he had no food.

3. The son got a job feeding pigs. He worked hard, but he was still hungry. He said, "If I go home, at least I won't starve. I was wrong to leave."

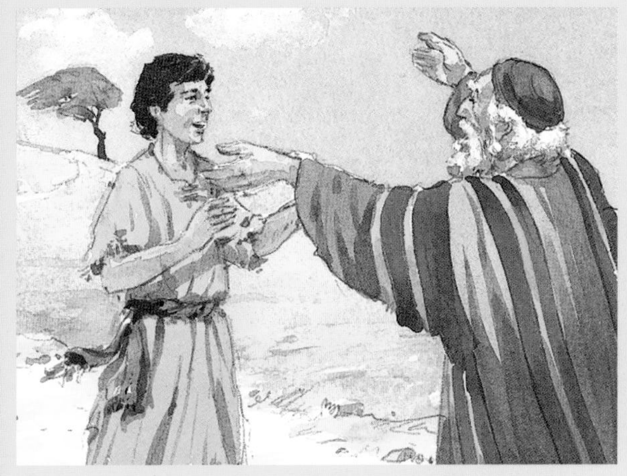

4. When the father saw his son, he shouted, "My son is home! Let's celebrate." Jesus said that, just like the father in His story, God forgives people.

The Library Book

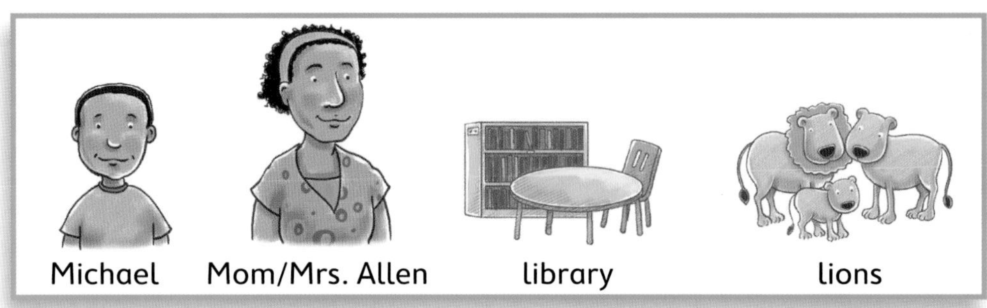

 brought home a  book for . It was about .

 read the book over and over. He really liked a picture of baby .

 One day  said, "Your  book is due. Please get it so I can take it back."

 looked at the picture of the baby . He wanted that picture. He tore it out of the book.

 As soon as  tore out the picture, he knew it was wrong.

 showed the book to his .

 said, "I'm sad you tore the  book. We'll have to pay for it. But first you need to ask God to forgive you for doing wrong."

 said, "Dear God, I'm sorry for tearing the book. Please forgive me. In Jesus's name. Amen."

 Then said, "If you help me pick up the toys, I'll help you pay for the  book."

 was happy to pick up the toys. He was thankful to get another chance to make a good choice.

The Father Who Forgave His Son

Bible story based on Luke 15:11–24

In the Bible story, Jesus told a story about a father who had two sons. What did the younger son ask for? What happened to this son? When he went back home, what did his father do? How is God like that father to us?

What did Mrs. Allen bring home for her son? What was the book about? What did Michael do to the book? Why? Michael had to earn money to pay for the book. But what else did he do? Will God forgive us when we make a mistake and we tell Him we're sorry?

You can probably each remember a time when you made a mistake. Feel free to share some of those right now. We know that no one is perfect and that sometimes we're going to make mistakes. But if we're truly sorry, we can pray to God and ask for forgiveness. God does forgive us when we do wrong.

What We Learned about God: God forgives us when we do wrong.

Let's Pray: Dear God, oh, how we wish we didn't make mistakes! When we do make them, please help us to quickly ask for forgiveness from those we've hurt and from You. Help us think through our choices more carefully, Lord, so we can learn from our mistakes. Thank You for loving us and for showing us how to forgive, because You forgive us. Amen.

Forgive as the Lord forgave you.
Colossians 3:13

Jesus Raises Lazarus

Bible story based on John 11:1–45

1. One day a man came to tell Jesus some sad news. He said, "Jesus, Your friend Lazarus is sick."

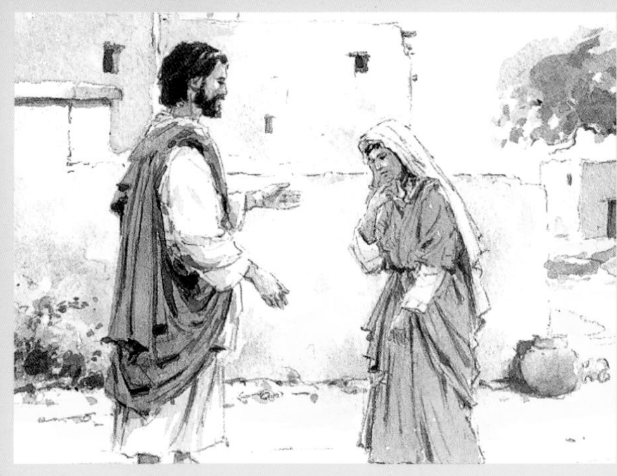

2. Jesus went to see Lazarus and his sisters. One sister, Martha, came running to Jesus, crying as she said, "Lazarus is dead."

3. Jesus said, "Where is Lazarus now?" Then Jesus went with Mary and Martha to the tomb where Lazarus was buried. Jesus cried.

4. But then Jesus made something great happen. Jesus shouted, "Lazarus, come out!" Lazarus was alive again! Jesus is all-powerful!

The Best Player

and  were playing outside.  saw  with a  .  and  watched as  threw the 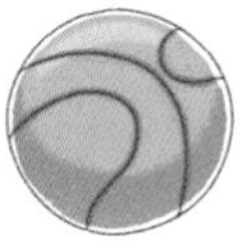 through the  hoop over and over again.

Just then  came outside. "  ," asked  , "will we ever play  like  ?"

"You'll have to get bigger and stronger," said  .

"Then you'll be more powerful."

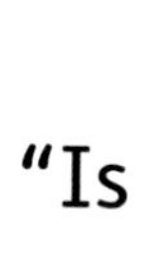“Is  the most powerful player? Is he the best 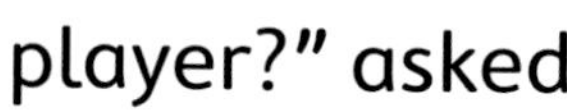player?” asked .

 said, “He’s good. But there are things he can’t do.”

“I know!” said . “He can’t help us when we pray. Only  can do that!”

 added, “ can do anything. He’s the best.  is all-powerful.”

Family Talk Time

Jesus Raises Lazarus

Bible story based on John 11:1–45

In the Bible story, what sad news did a man tell Jesus? When Jesus went to the tomb with Mary and Martha, what did He do? It was a miracle!

When Kaden and Isaac were playing outside, who were they watching? What was he doing? What did the boys wish they could do? Who did they realize was the best at everything?

Take some time together to name the different talents each of you has. Who in your family is good at sports? What about school? How about art or music? What else? God made each of us with special gifts and abilities. It's easy to think about God the way we think about ourselves, as if He is good at some things but not so good at other things. But God can do anything! He is the best at everything. And He will lead us and guide us so we can be the best we can be too.

What We Learned about God: Jesus is all-powerful.

Let's Pray: Lord Jesus, You are amazing and all-powerful. Help us remember that every gift and ability we have comes from You. You understand us, even though we're very different from one another. And we know that You are all-powerful. Nothing is impossible with You. Thank You, Lord, for loving us and for creating us with our own abilities and talents. Help us remember to honor You with them. Amen.

For no word from God will ever fail.
Luke 1:37

One Man Remembers to Thank Jesus

Bible story based on Luke 17:11–19

1. One day ten sick men saw Jesus walking toward them. The men were lepers. They had bad sores on their skin. They had to live outside their town.

2. The sick men called out, "Jesus, please help us." Jesus told the men they could go back into town. He didn't say so, but He had made the men well!

3. The men started toward town. They looked at their skin and saw that the sores were gone! Now they could live with their families again.

4. One man came back. He said, "Thank You, Jesus." He remembered to thank Jesus for His care.

Where Did Peanut Go?

Dear Jesus, please help us find Peanut. In Your name. Amen.

Peanut! You're here! Thank You, Jesus!
Meow!

Family Talk Time

One Man Remembers to Thank Jesus

Bible story based on Luke 17:11–19

In the Bible story, how many sick men called out to Jesus for help? What did Jesus tell them to do? As they were walking back to town, what happened to their sores? How many men came back to thank Jesus?

When Mia was helping her dad, what happened? What did they do as a way to help them find Peanut?

As a family, think of how God has taken care of you. Create a simple photo book of your family's favorite memories. This book can remind you of how Jesus has cared for your family through the years. At the back of the book, add a page that says "Thank You, Jesus, for caring for us."

What We Learned about God: Remember to thank Jesus for His care.

Let's Pray: Dear Jesus, like the one man in the Bible story and like Mia and her dad, we need to remember to thank You. We know You help us. We're so grateful that time after time, You have taken care of our family. You have helped us through some hard times, and You have also blessed us in incredible ways. Thank You, Jesus, for caring for us. Amen.

Give thanks to the LORD, for he is good;
his love endures forever.
1 Chronicles 16:34

Jesus Blesses the Children

Bible story based on Mark 10:13–16

1. Many people came to hear Jesus tell about God's love. The children wanted to see Jesus too.

2. Jesus's disciples told the children to go away. They said Jesus was too busy for children. But they were wrong!

3. Jesus said, "Let the children come to Me. God loves children very much. Learn how to love Me and be happy from the children."

4. Jesus hugged the children and prayed for them. The children were happy Jesus was their friend.

Kaden's Friends

 felt sad. He had no one to play with. Everyone was busy.

But knew  always had time for him. He said,

"Dear , I feel sad."

Soon,  saw . He had a .

 ran to . said, "I was talking to .

I was sad. Everyone is busy. There is no one to play with."

 said, "We can read my Bible  together.

 and  sat down to read.

 Soon,  brought out a plate of warm . 
and  thanked  for the . told
, "I'm glad you and  are my friends!"

Jesus Blesses the Children

Bible story based on Mark 10:13–16

In the Bible story, who wanted to visit with Jesus? Did Jesus let them? Are children important to Jesus? How did Jesus show them He was their friend?

Why was Kaden sad? Who did he find to play with? What did they do? What did Evan's mom give them to eat? Kaden said he was glad—for what?

When we think about friends, who comes to mind for you? Share with each other the names of some of your friends. What do you like about your friends? What do you do together? Now take time to think about Jesus. He is also your friend. Do you think of Him that way? Why or why not? How can you spend time with your friend Jesus this week?

What We Learned about God: Jesus is our special friend.

Let's Pray: Dear Jesus, thank You for being our friend. Please help us spend more time with You. We can read the Bible, pray, go to church, and spend time thinking about You and talking about You as a family. All of us have different friends, but help us remember that You are a friend to our whole family. We can talk to You and spend time with You together. We love You, Jesus. Amen.

A friend loves at all times.
Proverbs 17:17

Jesus Loves Zacchaeus

Bible story based on Luke 19:1–10

1. Jesus was coming down the road. Zacchaeus wanted to see Jesus. But Zacchaeus was short, and no one would let him be in front so he could see Jesus. Most people didn't like Zacchaeus.

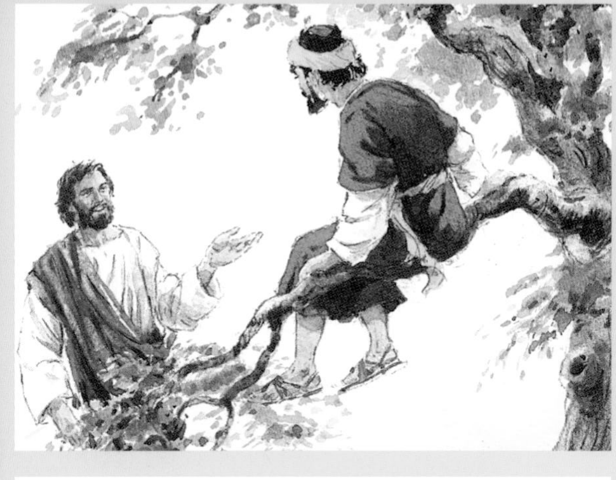

2. Zacchaeus decided to climb a tree. When Jesus saw the short man in the tree, He said, "Zacchaeus, come down. I'm going to your house."

3. The people grumbled, "Why does Jesus love Zacchaeus? No one else likes him!"

4. But Zacchaeus knew that Jesus loved him even when no one else did.

Sophia's Grumpy Day

It was a bad day. At breakfast  had a glass of  . When  tried to pour some, the  was gone.  said she would buy more  .  felt grumpy.

 wanted to play outside.  said  could play outside when it stopped raining, but the rain didn't stop.

Then  wanted to watch a  .  said she could watch her  after  , but  felt grumpy.

Finally  said, "Nobody loves me."

 looked sad. She prayed, "Dear , help  remember You love her and forgive her.  and I love her too. In 's name. Amen."

" really does love me,"  said. "And so do you and . I'm sorry for being grumpy, " she added.

"We forgive you," said  and .

Jesus Loves Zacchaeus

Bible story based on Luke 19:1-10

In the Bible story, who was coming down the road? Zacchaeus (Za-KEE-us) wanted to see Him; why couldn't he? So what did he do? Did Jesus see him? What happened next? Even though other people didn't like Zacchaeus, how did Jesus feel about him?

In the story about the Lopez family, do you remember who was having a bad day? What were some of the things that went wrong for Sophia? What did she think? Why wasn't it true? Will Jesus always love us?

We all have bad days. Sometimes our bad days are at home or at school or at the store. They can happen anywhere! Even when we make mistakes or feel grumpy like Sophia did, Jesus loves you, and so does your family. The bad day will pass by, and better days will come. And guess what. Jesus loves you on the good days too. He loves you no matter what!

You can do the activity at the back of the book as a reminder for how to show that you care about each other, no matter what!

What We Learned about God: Jesus loves us, no matter what.

Let's Pray: Dear Jesus, thank You for showing us what real love is. It doesn't matter if we're having a bad day or a good day, You will always love us. Help us show that love to each other as a family. Help us listen to each other when we need to talk. Help us cheer another person up who is feeling down. Help us remember that nothing is impossible with You. Amen.

My grace is sufficient for you,
for my power is made perfect in weakness.
2 Corinthians 12:9

People Praise Jesus as Their King

Bible story based on Luke 19:29–38; John 12:12–19

1. Many people were going to Jerusalem to worship God. Jesus told two disciples, "Go to the next town. Find a donkey and bring it here."

2. The disciples found the donkey where Jesus said it would be. They told the owners, "The Lord needs it." The owners let them take it.

3. The disciples brought the donkey to Jesus. The donkey had no saddle. So the disciples put their coats on its back and helped Jesus get on.

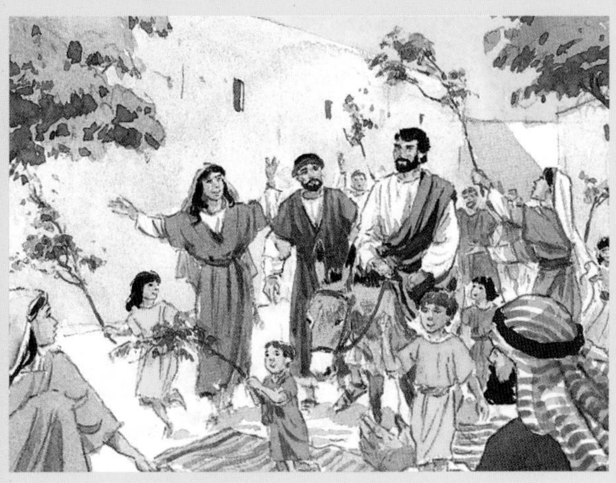

4. The people along the road praised Jesus as their King. They put their coats on the road, waved branches, and shouted, "Hosanna!"

Praising Jesus

 liked to .

"Is it a picture of ?" asked .

"Yes," said . "Do you see the people praising Him?"

"We learned a song about praising  at ," said . As he started to ,  got up from her chair and started talking to .

"Stop!" said . "I can't  and praise  while you two are talking."

"  loves  too," said  . "Would you like to  with Evan?" So they sang the song together.

"I know another way we can praise  ," said  . "At  , we march around the room while we  ."

" would like that, and  would too," said  , "because  loves all the different ways we praise Him."

So they marched around the room and sang another song. Then  asked if he could  a picture of  too.

Family Talk Time

People Praise Jesus as Their King

Bible story based on Luke 19:29–38; John 12:12–19

In the Bible story, what did Jesus ask the two disciples to bring Him? Then what did Jesus do? What did the people wave in the air? And what word did they say over and over?

What kind of song did Evan sing? What was the problem? How did Mrs. Li respond to the problem? What was another way that the children praised Jesus?

When Jesus rode on a donkey, it was the beginning of Holy Week. Many important things happened during this week. Talk about these things as a family. There was the gathering of Jesus with the disciples in the upper room, where Jesus washed their feet. And then they celebrated the very first Lord's Supper, or Communion. Then Judas left the gathering and betrayed Jesus. That same night Jesus was praying in the garden of Gethsemane, and the soldiers came and took him away. Jesus went to Pontius Pilate and was beaten. Then He died on the cross, even though He had done nothing wrong. Jesus is our Savior, because He saved us from our sins. Hosanna!

What We Learned about God: We should praise Jesus!

Let's Pray: Hosanna to the King of kings! Thank You, Jesus, for saving us from our sins. Even though You did nothing wrong, You chose to die on a cross for us. We praise You, Lord, our God. And we look forward to seeing You in heaven someday. Amen.

Jesus Christ is the same yesterday and today and forever.
Hebrews 13:8

Jesus Answers Questions

Bible story based on Mark 12:28–34

Some people were standing around Jesus. They were asking Him questions. They were all saying, "I have a question. I have a question."

One man stepped up to Jesus. He said, "Jesus, can You tell us which of God's rules is most important?"

Jesus answered, "The most important rule is to love God with all your heart."

That meant people should love God more than anyone or anything else in the world.

Then Jesus said, "The second most important rule is to love each other." Jesus explained that people should love others just as much as they love themselves.

The man knew that Jesus's answer was good. Loving God and loving each other are God's most important rules.

The Most Important Rule

It was the first morning of church day camp, and there was so much to do. Mia and Sophia wanted to do everything. But first, all the kids and the leaders met together.

When the girls sat down on the bench, they saw all their friends from church. And there was a surprise! Mr. Wood, their teacher from school, was standing in front of the group. He was talking to the children just as he did at school.

Then Mr. Wood told the kids the rules. He said, "The first rule is the most important rule at camp. You must stay with your group at all times. Then your leader will know where you are." Mia and Sophia listened to all the rules. There was a lot to remember.

Next, Mr. Wood read the names of the leaders and the children in each group. Sophia and Mia were in different groups.

"I wish you were in my group," Sophia told Mia.

"Me, too," agreed Mia. "But maybe we can sit together at lunch."

The girls had fun all morning making crafts, playing games, and listening to a Bible story. At lunchtime, Mia and Sophia got to eat at the same table. They talked all about the things they had done. Sophia said, "My group is going swimming next. Come with us."

Mia loved to swim, so when the groups started to line up, Mia followed Sophia to her group. But then Mia heard her leader counting all the children in her group.

"I had better go with my group," Mia said to Sophia. "My leader will be worried when she can't find me. And Mr. Wood said that staying with your group is the most important camp rule."

Sophia looked sad as Mia walked back to her group, but Mia was right. She needed to stay with her group. Later that day, Mia and Sophia sat together near the campfire and roasted marshmallows. Camp was fun!

Jesus Answers Questions

Bible story based on Mark 12:28–34

In the Bible story, what did Jesus say was the most important rule? And what was the second most important rule? That's right! Loving God and loving each other are the most important rules!

Where were Mia and Sophia? What rules were they learning about? Why was it hard for them to follow the rules? But were they glad they did? Why?

As a family, you have rules that you all follow. What are some of those rules? Why do you have those rules for your home? What is the most important rule at your house? Does it have to do how you treat each other? What about loving God? Is that important at your house too?

What We Learned about God: We should love God and each other.

Let's Pray: Dear God, thank You for giving us rules to follow. Sometimes they are hard, but we know that Your rules will help us live in a way that pleases You. Help us always remember what is most important—loving You and loving each other as much as we love ourselves. Amen.

Love your neighbor as yourself.
Mark 12:31

A Special Offering

Bible story based on Mark 12:41–44

Kerplunk, clink, jingle went the coins into the offering box. As Jesus rested outside at the temple, He watched people give their offerings.

A man with fancy clothes dropped many big coins into the box. *Kerplunk, kerplunk.* Other people came with big coins that made a lot of noise too.

Then Jesus saw a woman come to the temple yard. Her husband had died. She had very little money, but she dropped her offering into the box. *Clink, clink.* Two little coins. It wasn't much money, but it was all she had.

Jesus said, "This poor woman has given more than all of the rich people. They gave only a part of their money, but she gave everything she had."

Blankets for India

I saved ten dollars so I could buy Mom a special gift this year. If I give money to buy a blanket, I won't have money to buy Mom's gift.
Remember our story from Sunday school when the widow gave everything she had?

I decided to give my whole ten dollars to buy a blanket. God will be happy I gave everything I had. I'll make Mom a gift.
Blankets for India

Family Talk Time

A Special Offering

Bible story based on Mark 12:41–44

In the Bible story, where was Jesus? What was He watching people do? When a poor woman gave her offering, what did Jesus say about it?

Remember the Parker family? What special job did they do? What were the children going to do to help the hospital where Dr. Parker will work? What did Sophia decide to do?

As a family, talk about what an offering means. What does an offering help pay for at church? Does an offering always mean giving money? What are some other ways we can give an offering? Does the amount of the offering matter? What is more important?

What We Learned about God: God's people give their offering.

Let's Pray: Dear God, thank You for taking care of us. You have blessed our family with so much. Thank You for a warm place to live, for the beds that we sleep in, for the food that we eat. Help us have generous hearts as we think about how we can give our offerings. Even when we may not have a lot of money, help us find ways to give to You, Lord. Help our hearts to be giving, like the poor woman in the Bible story. Amen.

God loves a cheerful giver.
2 Corinthians 9:7

Jesus Washes His Disciples' Feet

Bible story based on John 13:1–17, 34–35

1. One night, Jesus and His disciples were planning to have a special meal together. Two of the disciples fixed special food and a special table.

2. Jesus and His disciples sat around the table. Jesus knew He was going back to heaven soon. He wanted to show how much He loved His disciples.

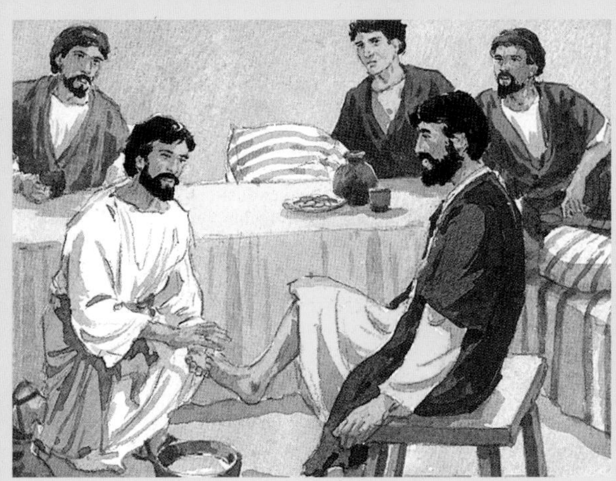

3. Jesus got a towel and some water. He poured water into a bowl and began to wash His disciples' feet. He dried their feet with the towel.

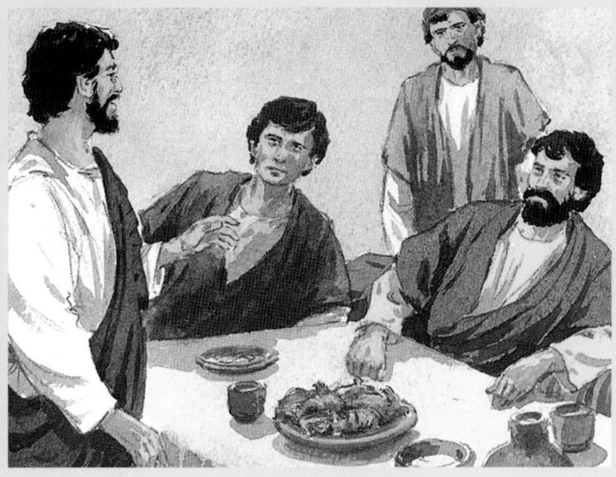

4. The disciples were surprised that Jesus wanted to wash their dirty feet. Jesus said, "I want you to show love to others as I showed love to you."

Captain Kind

I help my sister, Ava, tie her shoes.
I help Mom when I set the table for her.
When my brother, Caleb, has a lot of homework, I fix a snack for him after school.

Those are good things! It's good to show love to others. What do you think, Kaden?
Ahoy! I am Captain Kind! I no longer look for gold. I look for ways to show love.

Family Talk Time

Jesus Washes His Disciples' Feet

Bible story based on John 13:1–17, 34–35

In the Bible story, Jesus and His disciples were getting ready to have the very first celebration of the Lord's Supper (or Communion). Soon Jesus would be going to die on the cross to save us from our sins. And this was a way to remember what He did for us. Before the Lord's Supper, what did Jesus do to the disciples' feet? Why did He do that? And what did He want them to remember to do as well?

In the comic strip, who was Kaden pretending to be? What are some ways that the children showed love to their families? What did Kaden change his pretend name to? Why?

As a family, talk about ways that you show love to each other at home. It feels great to show other people love, doesn't it? How does showing love to each other help your family understand Jesus's love?

What I Learned about God: Jesus shows us His love.

Let's Pray: Dear Jesus, You showed amazing love when You washed the disciples' feet. But You showed even more love when You died on the cross to save us from our sins. Thank You for this sacrifice. Help us show love to others, and may we help them learn about Your love too.

[Jesus said,] "Anyone who has seen me has seen the Father."
John 14:9

Go Tell the Others, "Jesus Lives!"

Bible story based on Matthew 27:33–38, 57–61; 28:1–8

Some people put Jesus on a cross to die. A friend named Joseph buried Jesus in a tomb. Joseph rolled a big stone in front of the tomb.

On the third day, two women went to the tomb. They were shocked to see the tomb open and an angel sitting there!

The angel said, "Do not be afraid. I know you are looking for Jesus. He is not here. He is alive."

The women saw that Jesus was no longer dead. They knew He was alive.

The angel told the women, "Go quickly to tell His disciples that Jesus lives."

The women ran to tell others that Jesus lives.

Surprises!

I'm excited! Grandpa and Grandma should be here soon!
We can show them our surprise before we go to church together.
I think I see their car now!
Hi, Grandma and Grandpa! Close your eyes!
We're going to lead you to our surprise!
Open your eyes to see our surprise!
Are those the flowers we helped you plant last year?
Yes! You told us they would come up again. But they were buried in the snow all winter. We thought they were dead.
I love to see flowers in the spring. They remind me of the day that Jesus came alive again.
What do you mean?
Your flowers were buried in the ground. But they grew again. Jesus's body was buried in a tomb. But He didn't stay buried. He came back to life again.

We have a surprise for you, too.
Close your eyes.
I'll go get it.

Here's our surprise!
Let's put those flowers on the table. Every time we see them, we can remember how happy we are that Jesus is alive!

Go Tell the Others, "Jesus Lives!"

Bible story based on Matthew 27:33–38, 57–61; 28:1–8

Who was the person who buried Jesus in a tomb? What did he roll in front of the tomb? On the third day, two women went to the tomb. What did they see that shocked them? Who was sitting on top of the big stone? What did the angel tell them? What did the women do?

When Grandma and Grandpa Young came over for Easter, what did the children show them outside? Why are flowers a reminder of how Jesus died and rose again? What present did the grandparents give?

Jesus lives! What a message to share! The angel told the two women. They told Jesus's disciples. The Young family shared flowers to tell each other that Jesus is alive. How can your family share the message that Jesus lives? Praise God as a family that Jesus lives!

What We Learned about God: We can tell others that Jesus lives!

Let's Pray: Dear God, thank You for sending Your Son, Jesus, to save us. We can now go to heaven someday to be with You. And we want as many other people as possible to believe in You so they can go to heaven someday too. Help each one of us show Your love to others. Give us the courage to tell others about Jesus. Amen.

Christ lives in me.
Galatians 2:20

Jesus Goes to Heaven

Bible story based on Luke 24:50–53; Acts 1:7–11; Romans 8:31–39

1. One day Jesus and His friends went to a hill. Jesus blessed His disciples so they would know that He would always love them.

2. When Jesus was done talking, He began to go up. A cloud hid Him. He went up, up, up into heaven.

3. Two angels came. They said, "Jesus is living in heaven now. But someday He will come back again."

4. Jesus's friends went back to the city. They were glad that Jesus was alive in heaven. They wanted to tell everyone that Jesus always loves us.

Saying Goodbye

Don't go, Grandma. I don't want you to leave.
Kaden, we will miss you and your siblings, but we will only be gone two weeks.

Maybe you'll forget us. Maybe you won't come back.
We could never forget you! We don't forget people we love just because we go away.

We'll call you when we get to the mountains. We'll even send postcards, so you know we didn't forget you.
And we'll pray for Grandma and Grandpa every day, just like we always do.

But, Grandpa, who will feed Golden Boy and all the other farm animals?
You can help your dad feed Golden Boy. Madison can help feed Pepper and the other animals too. The animals will be fine.

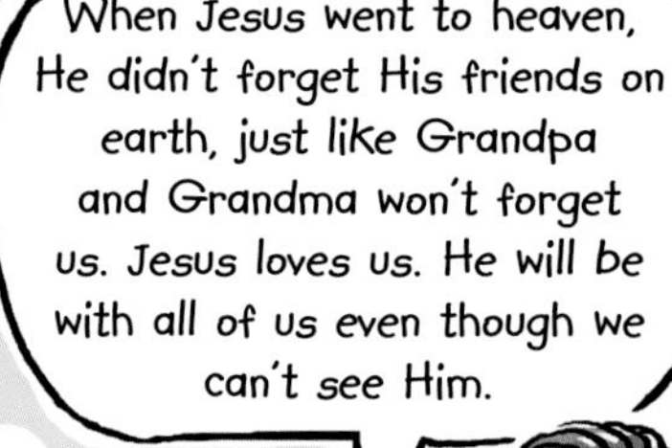

When Jesus went to heaven, He didn't forget His friends on earth, just like Grandpa and Grandma won't forget us. Jesus loves us. He will be with all of us even though we can't see Him.

I get it! We won't be able to see Grandma and Grandpa, but they'll still love us, like Jesus does.

Grandma, I want to give you and Grandpa a good-bye kiss.

We'll be waiting for a postcard! And we won't forget you love us.

Jesus Goes to Heaven

Bible story based on Luke 24:50–53; Acts 1:7–11; Romans 8:31–39

One day Jesus and His disciples went to a hill. What did Jesus want the disciples to remember? When Jesus was done talking, what happened? Then two angels appeared. What did they say? Is Jesus coming back? Who did the disciples tell about this?

Why were Madison and Kaden sad? What were they worried about? But why didn't they need to worry? Why did Mrs. Young remind them about when Jesus went to heaven?

Think about the last time a close relative or friend came to visit your family. What were some fun times you shared together? It's always hard when it's time to say good-bye, but no matter what, you know they won't forget you, and you won't forget them. It's like that with Jesus. Even though He left this world and went back up to heaven a long time ago, He still knows us and loves us. He hasn't forgotten us. And someday He will come back again!

What We Learned about God: Jesus will always love us.

Let's Pray: Dear Jesus, thank You for loving us. We know that You see all the different parts of our lives and that You care about all of them. When we're sad or are missing the people we love, please be near to us, Lord. And help us help each other when we're lonely. Help us remind each other that we are loved and that You will always love us. Amen.

Therefore go and make disciples of all nations.
Matthew 28:19

God Sent Philip to Teach His Word

Bible story based on Acts 8:4–5, 26–39

1. Philip loved God very much. God asked Philip to teach people about Him and His Son, Jesus.

2. One day God sent Philip to a certain road. Philip walked along the road.

3. Philip saw a man sitting in a chariot. God told Philip to go up to the man. The man was reading a Bible scroll.

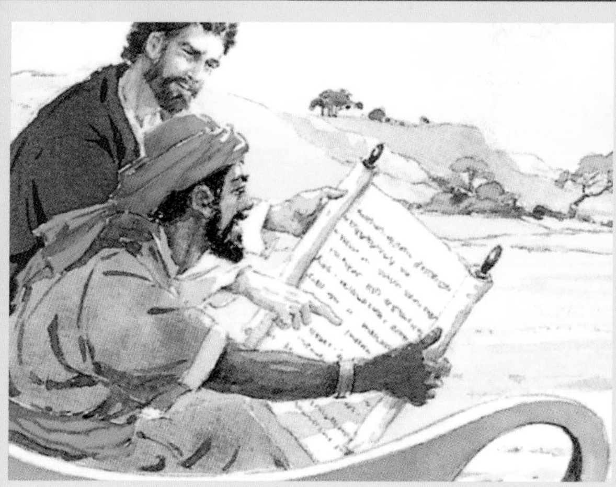

4. Philip taught the man that the words on the Bible scroll were about Jesus. The man believed in Jesus, God's Son.

The Big Question

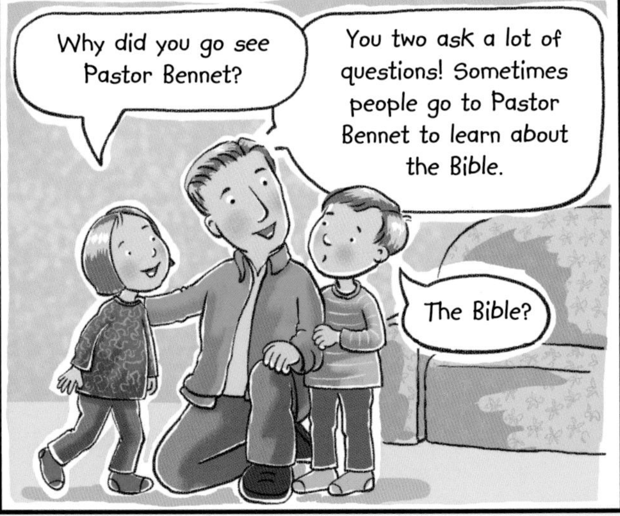

A man who often comes into the sandwich shop asked me a question about the Bible. I didn't know the answer, so I went to see Pastor Bennet.

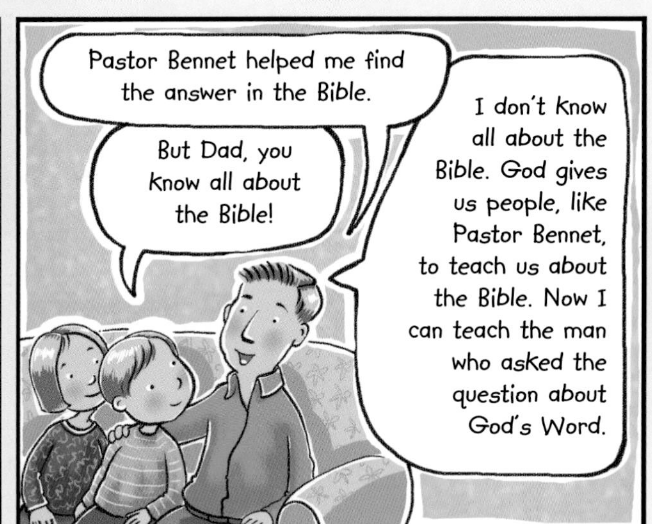
Pastor Bennet helped me find the answer in the Bible.
But Dad, you know all about the Bible!
I don't know all about the Bible. God gives us people, like Pastor Bennet, to teach us about the Bible. Now I can teach the man who asked the question about God's Word.

God Sent Philip to Teach His Word

Bible story based on Acts 8:4–5; 26–39

In the Bible story, a man named Philip helped teach people about Jesus. When he was walking down the road one day, who did he see sitting in a chariot? What was the man reading? What did Philip explain to this man? Did the man then believe in Jesus?

When Kaden and Madison were playing a game, who rushed out the door? Why did he go see Pastor Bennet? Who had asked Mr. Young a question about the Bible?

Now that you've completed this book as a family, you have learned more about God and the Bible. Share what your favorite story was and why. Spend some extra time together thinking back over this experience. The stories in this book may be finished, but God's story keeps on going and going! How are you going to keep learning and growing in your faith? Talk about this together. Do you know some people outside your family who can help you learn more about the Bible? Who are they?

What We Learned about God: God gives us people to teach us His Word.

Let's Pray: Dear God, thank You for all the teachers you have brought into our lives who have helped us learn about You. And thank You for being with us as we've learned about You in this Bible storybook. Help us remember these stories and, more important, help us remember how to live out our faith as a family. We ask that You use each one of us in mighty ways to tell others about Jesus and the Bible. Amen.

As I have loved you, so you must love one another.
John 13:34

Good Job! You Did It!

 loves all of the people and all of the families you have read about in . And loves your family too.

You can keep reading about  and God's amazing grace.

Where? In the !

Additional Activities

God Made Plants for Our World

(pages 15–18)

Activity Suggestion: I Spy Nature Bingo

As a family, take a walk through your neighborhood or go to a nearby park. Use the nature bingo sheets below to help you find some of the plants God created. If the weather or something else this week prevents you from taking a walk, look through a picture book, magazine, or go online to find the plants.

I Spy Nature Bingo

Red flowers	Blades of grass	Rough tree bark
Veins on a leaf	Flower with five petals	Pointy-edged leaf
Bush with flowers	Branch with thorns	Fruit tree

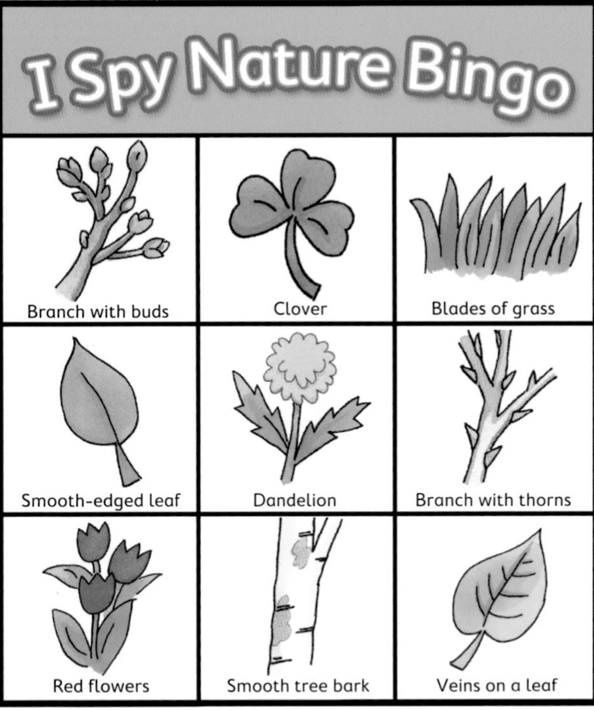

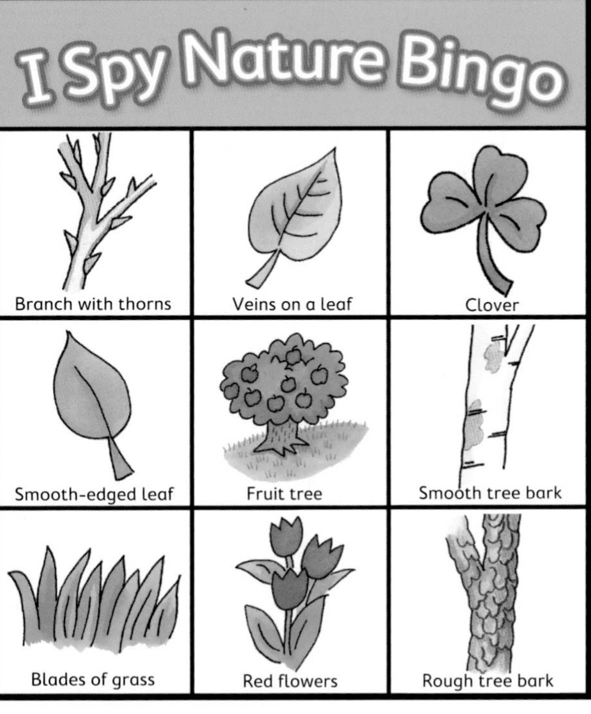

Jesus Is Baptized

(pages 115–118)

Activity Suggestion: "I Belong" Water Bottles

When Jesus was baptized, He showed that He belonged to God. Make these water bottles as a fun way to show whose family you belong to. You can put something similar on each water bottle, such as a cross sticker. And then put your own personal touches on your bottle. Decorate mugs or cups instead of water bottles, if you prefer.

You will need:

Reusable water bottles

Decorative items such as stickers, ribbon, permanent markers, pictures from magazines, stained glass paint, puff paint, etc.

Decoupage glue or clear, wide packing tape

Paint sealer (if you use paint)

Old shirts to protect clothes

To make your water bottle:

1. Clean your water bottle and let it dry.
2. Decorate the outside of the water bottle. Don't decorate near where you will drink out of it.
3. Cover your decoration with decoupage glue or packing tape to keep your designs safe. Decoupage glue will go on white but will dry clear.
4. If you painted your water bottle, cover the paint with paint sealer.
5. Make sure your artwork is dry before you use the water bottle.

Jesus Teaches about Prayer

(pages 159–162)

Activity Suggestion: Prayer Chart

Use your Prayer Chart to help you remember to pray to our loving God. Color each box or put a sticker in it when you pray about each thing.

	Sunday	Monday	Tuesday	Wednesday	Thursday	Friday	Saturday
Praise God.							
Thank God for giving you what you need.							
Ask God to forgive you.							
Ask God to help you do good things and say no to bad things.							
In Jesus's name. Amen.							

Jesus Loves Zacchaeus

(pages 183–186)

Activity Suggestion: Love Bandages

Create personal adhesive bandages that will remind each member of your family that Jesus loves us and forgives us. Put the bandages in an accessible place for the family to use throughout the week as a reminder that Jesus loves them. Have fun finding ways to share bandages—they're not just for physical bumps and bruises!

You will need:

One box of plain adhesive bandages (assorted sizes)

Fine or ultra-fine point permanent markers

Small heart stickers

Old shirts to protect clothes

To make your bandages:

1. Cover clothes with old shirts as needed. Permanent marker can't be washed out of clothing.
2. Give each family member some bandages. Decorate the bandages with hearts, stickers, and words like "Jesus loves you" and "Jesus forgives you."
3. Let the bandages dry before putting them in the box.
4. Have all family members use the bandages throughout the week to let each other, and friends, know that Jesus loves them and forgives them. Give them out to cover physical hurts and heal emotional pains. Share about Zacchaeus and Jesus when you put on a bandage.

The LORD bless you and keep you;
the LORD make His face shine upon you
and be gracious to you;
the LORD turn His face toward you and give you peace.

Numbers 6:24–26